J. Carpenter Smith

History of St. George's Parish

J. Carpenter Smith

History of St. George's Parish

ISBN/EAN: 9783337373153

Printed in Europe, USA, Canada, Australia, Japan

Cover: Foto ©ninafisch / pixelio.de

More available books at **www.hansebooks.com**

HISTORY

OF

SAINT GEORGE'S PARISH

FLUSHING, LONG ISLAND

BY

J. CARPENTER SMITH, S. T. D.

FLUSHING

ST. GEORGE'S SWORD AND SHIELD

1897

PREFACE

The following history of Saint George's Parish, with the exception of the first and the last chapters, has been compiled from a series of articles written for SAINT GEORGE'S SWORD AND SHIELD by the rector of the parish— the Rev. J. Carpenter Smith, S. T. D. The editor's work has been to condense and arrange the material thus furnished. He has not undertaken to verify, by independent research, dates or statements of historic fact. The history appears in the fiftieth year of Dr. Smith's rectorship. The publishers beg that it may be accepted as their offering to commemorate this half-century of faithful service.

The editor is indebted to the Rt. Rev. William Stevens Perry, D. D., LL. D., for several illustrations which have been taken from his HISTORY OF THE AMERICAN EPISCOPAL CHURCH; to friends and relatives of former rectors, for help in securing portraits; to Miss J. L. Delafield, for the portrait of Francis Lewis; and also to Mr. E. A. Fairchild for assistance in preparing the following pages for publication.

Whitsun-tide, 1897.   H. D. W.

THE HISTORY

OF SAINT GEORGE'S PARISH.

CHAPTER I.

THE FIRST SETTLEMENT AND EARLY HISTORY OF FLUSHING.*

LONG ISLAND was known by many different names before its present one was accepted. The last to be discarded and forgotten was Nassau Island, which is the name we find in our parish charter.

That portion of the Island which now comprises the town of Flushing was originally held by the Matinecoe (or Martinecock) tribe of Indians and was purchased from them by the Dutch. At the time when our history begins—about the middle of the seventeenth century— the English held the eastern part of the Island, while the western half was under the control of the Dutch. In 1641 the Dutch Governor and Council agreed to allow the English to settle on Long Island if they would take the oath of allegiance to the States General and the Dutch West India Company. The towns of Hempstead, Flushing, Jamaica and Newtown were originally settled by the English under these conditions. Flushing was first set-

*Wood's Settlement of Towns of Long Island. Flint's Early Long Island.

tled in the year 1645 by "a band of English planters who
had lived in Holland. They came hither from Lynn."
A patent for sixteen thousand acres was made out to
Thomas Ffarington, John Lawrence, John Townsend and
others. They called their possession Vlissingen, after
the Dutch town. The name afterwards appears as Vliss-
ing, and finally, Flushing.

These English settlers became Dutch subjects and were
permitted to hold land, enjoy the liberty of conscience
and choose their own magistrates, subject to the approval
of the Governor. The magistrates were empowered to
hold court—civil and criminal—and to make ordinances
for the government of the town. The first charter of
Flushing gave the inhabitants authority to elect only a
Schout, or constable, who had power to preserve order
and was to report all cases of importance to the Governor.
Later magistrates were given to Flushing as to the other
towns. The rule of the Dutch government was regarded
as tyrannical, and in 1653 a convention of delegates from
Brooklyn, Flatbush, Flatlands, Gravesend, Newtown,
Flushing and Hempstead was held, to protest against
what they deemed arbitrary rule. Nothing was accomplished by this protest and in 1662, at a meeting held at
Hempstead, the towns agreed to put themselves under
the jurisdiction of Connecticut. This never came to pass,
for two years later, in 1664, the Colony of New Neth-
erland was surrendered to the Crown of Great Britain.
In 1673 the Dutch again gained possession, and in the
following year, 1674, the Colony finally passed under the
control of the English.

The Rev. Francis Doughty, who is described as an
"ecclesiastical firebrand," was the first minister in Flushing. We read that his salary of six hundred guilders
was never paid. Mr. Doughty had been vicar of Sod-

bury, in England, and was silenced for non-conformity. He came to New England, but found—his son-in-law tells us--that he "had got out of the frying-pan into the fire." He came to Long Island in 1642 and settled at Mespat.

The first Quakers came to Flushing in 1657. Robert Hodgson was their leader. They, for some time, met with rough treatment at the hands of the Dutch—were

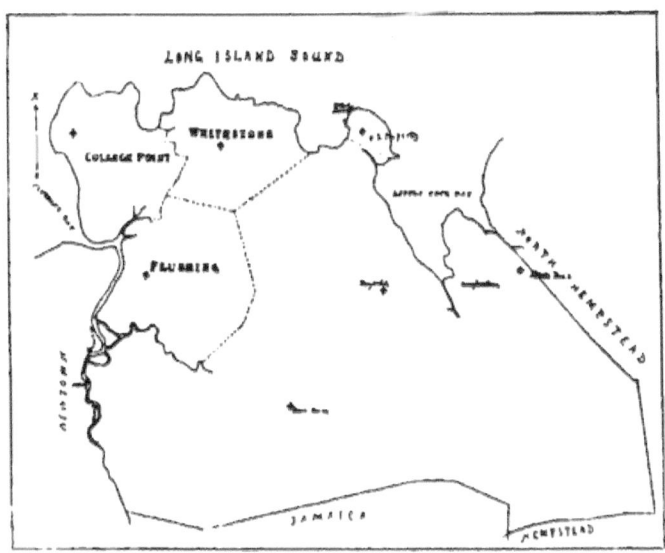

MAP OF FLUSHING. THE LOCATION OF A CHURCH OR CHAPEL
IS MARKED BY A CROSS.

fined and imprisoned. To shelter a Quaker for one night was an offence punishable with a fine of $50, and any vessel bringing Quakers to the Province was liable to be confiscated. In spite of all this the Friends increased.

Meetings were first held in the woods and when, in 1661, the Bowne house was built, it was used as their place of worship for over thirty years, Their founder,

George Fox, visited Flushing in 1672, and preached under the oaks opposite the Bowne House—where he was entertained during his visit. The Friends' Meeting House was built in 1695, and is still in a good state of preservation.

In 1660, some newly arrived Frenchmen settled in Flushing and began the industry of horticulture, for which the town has ever since been famous.

These are the various elements and influences that have made the Flushing we know.

There were no post offices on Long Island until 1793. The people of Kings and Queens counties received their mail at New York; Suffolk was served from New London. A post route was established in 1764 and mail was carried fortnightly along the North Shore by a horseman, who returned by the South Side.

The ownership of slaves was almost universal among the well-to-do, and there are few wills, up to the beginning of this century, that do not contain bequests of slaves. Slavery gradually disappeared in New York State after 1799, but there are, no doubt, negroes still living who were born in slavery on Long Island.

The town of Flushing extends from Flushing Creek, on the west, to the town of North Hempstead, on the east —a distance of about seven miles; and from the North Shore to the boundaries of the towns of Jamaica and Hempstead, on the south, about five miles. The ground is fertile and slightly undulating. The population in 1890 was 19,803. Within the town are the villages of Flushing, College Point, Whitestone, Bayside, Douglaston and Little Neck—all originally within St. George's parish.

CHAPTER II.

IN the year of our Lord 1702, Flushing was a quiet, farming hamlet, the majority of whose inhabitants were members of the Society of Friends, and the "Old Quaker Meeting House" was the only place of public worship. It was in this year that the first clergymen of the Church of England visited the village. The "Society for the Propagation of the Gospel in Foreign Parts," sent out the Rev. George Keith on a "preliminary mission of inquiry." He was to travel throughout the colonies, seek the scattered families of the Church and awaken the people to a sense of their religious duties. The selection was a happy one : Keith was pre-eminently fitted for the work. He had been a zealous follower of George Fox, and was the most learned of his supporters. He knew well the field. While a Quaker, he had been sent to the Colony of Pennsylvania to aid its founder, William Penn. He was a propagandist by nature. Tireless in zeal and energy, he was one of those men who are always found near the battle flag, where the fight is thickest and the work hardest. While a Friend, he was a distinguished travelling minister and had attended yearly meetings in Flushing and Oyster Bay. Discovering dangerous tendencies in the peculiar tenets of the Friends, and foreseeing their results, he severed his connection with them and returned to England, ultimately to take Holy Orders in the Church.

In April, 1702, he started on his mission to the Colonies. He came in an English warship, which brought the Governors of New England and New Jersey to their provinces. The Rev. John Talbot came with them as chaplain. With them also was the Rev. Patrick Gordon, who was sent out as missionary to Jamaica, L. I.

Mr. Talbot, the chaplain, became so enthusiastic about Keith and his mission, that he begged to become a fellow laborer and a companion in his travels. His proposal was accepted and in due time, at the solicitation of the Rev. Mr. Gordon, the Venerable Society appointed him Keith's assistant. Their ship reached Boston in June, 1702, and after a few days the two men began their journey. It is not our purpose to follow them from the Piscataway river, in New England, to the swamps and wilds of North Carolina They went from hamlet to hamlet and house to house, preaching wherever they could gain a hearing, baptizing hundreds, gathering the wandering sheep into organized folds, and making provision to build churches wherever that work could be done.

After this long missionary journey, they began a visitation to the waste places of Long Island. Keith knew well that Flushing was a stronghold of Quakerism. It was probably less than a score of years since he had visited the meeting there as an accepted ministering Friend. He knew the opposition which awaited him. This would not deter him—indeed, we suspect he would rather like it. As a canny Scotchman and quondam Quaker, he was a man of peace, i. e., when things around him made for peace, but when otherwise he could be equal to the emergency.

On a bright Thursday morning in September, 1702, Keith, in company with the Rev. William Vesey, Rector of New York, the Rev. John Talbot and some others,

REV. GEORGE KEITH.

entered the meeting-house—the same building which
still stands on Broadway. The Fifth day of the week,
as well as the First day, or Sunday, was then, as it
is now, the appointed day for meeting. Mr. Keith took
his seat in the preacher's gallery and awaited during
the solemn silence, which is an impressive form of the
Friends' worship. At the proper time he rose and began
to speak. He soon announced himself as a minister and
missionary of the Church of England, whom the Queen
and Bishops had sent to preach in the Colonies. A loud
protest and remonstrance followed on the part of the
Friends. Keith had no moral right to obtrude his services upon the Friends in their own meeting-house, contrary to their remonstrance. It was a breach of Christian

charity. But it was A. D. 1702, and not A. D. 1897. We
are not apologists for the disturbance, much less for
the disturber. But Keith had been a zealous disciple of
George Fox, and that eminent master and his early fol-
lowers in England had entered churches or "steeple
houses" and meeting houses, and obtruded their "testimony to the truth" upon unwilling congregations, under
the plea of a sense of duty.

The scene which followed was not to edification. It
was too much for even the peaceable spirit of the Friends.
The intruder was an apostate from the faith—a renegade
who now strove to destroy what he had formerly sought
to build up. His presence among them added insult to
injury.

Mr. Keith says that as soon as he began to speak he
"was so much interrupted by the clamor and noise of the
Quakers that he could not proceed. After this, one of
their speakers began to speak, and continued speaking
about an hour. The whole was a ramble of nonsense
and perversion of Scripture, with gross reflections on the
Church and the Government. When he had done he
went away in all haste. I stood up again in their meeting, but they made a new interruption, and threatened
me with being guilty of a breach of the Act of Toleration,
and that by so doing I had put myself in the Queen's debt
twenty pounds." In answer to this, Keith denied that he
had "interrupted their meeting, but had remained silent
all the time their speaker was speaking." They disputed
his right to speak in their meetings. Instead of resting
this denial on the rules and discipline of the Friends,
which Keith well knew, they appealed to the Act of Toleration. Keith saw his advantage and calmly told them
that he had a better right to speak there than any of their
speakers had. They expressed wonder and asked how

he could say that. They had bought the ground and built the meeting-house at their own expense, but he had contributed nothing. It was their own, not his. This appeal to common sense and justice seemed to arouse the already indignant Friends. One sprang up, and with as much heat as a Friend is allowed (the precise degree is a variable quantity), ordered him to go out of the house.

Mr. Keith replied : " None of your speakers have any right to speak in your meeting-houses, because you have not your meeting-houses licensed as the Act of Toleration requires. Nor have any of your preachers qualified themselves as that act expresses ; viz., to sign to thirty-four of the XXXIX Articles of the Church of England. This you have not done, nor can you do ; whereas I am qualified as the Act requires."

It would have been a cruel mockery to demand such subscription from a religious society like the Friends, yet such was the law in the Mother Country and in some of the Colonies. Keith and his opponents assumed that it was the law in the Province of New York. This was a debatable question, as the Church of England had not been formally established by the Provincial Assembly.

Notwithstanding the defeat of the Friends in this battle of words, they had yet a reserve to call to their aid. They abandoned the Act of Toleration as too dangerous in its recoil, and, through a venerable speaker, brought up the familiar charge of a " hireling ministry." "They accused me," Keith says, " that I came not in love to preach to them, but was hired by the Bishops to come, and that the love of money brought me to America, not the love of souls." It was the old charge which George Fox had made with great success and some truth. No doubt, at that time, to the shame of the Church and

the hurt of religion, there were among her clergy in England many who richly merited the odious title of "*hireling*" priests." But, according to a wise authority, "the
bearing of the observation is in the application of it."
It applies only where it is true. Keith's and his co-labor-
ers' small stipend, their abundant labors, their "journey-
ings oft" and dangerous, proved that a "ready mind" to
do good, and not a "love of filthy lucre," was the
power that brought them to the Colonies. Keith de-

QUAKER MEETING-HOUSE, BUILT 1695. ST. GEORGE'S CHURCH IN THE
DISTANCE.

clared the charge to be false. "It was true," he said,
"that God had raised up kind friends who assisted him
with money in his chargeable undertaking." In this he
had the example of the Apostle who was helped in his
journey. But this, he retorted, "was no more than the
Quakers in London did, who largely supplied the travelling Friends who come over from England to America,
with money out of their national stock, besides what
these travelling Friends gather from the several meetings

they visit in America." It is a well known fact that the
Friends did give pecuniary aid to their travelling ministers. Commissary Bray, when pleading for the unpaid
clergy of Maryland, urged upon the Society the fact, that
while the Quakers amply supported their travelling ministers the Church had left hers to starve. It was a paid
ministerial service after all, under whatever pretext or
name the money was given.

They replied that they never knew of any money given
by their meeting to any travelling Friend, and asked if he
had ever received any money from their meeting while
he was a travelling Friend among them. "Yes, said I,
from this very meeting I have received money." They
asked "of whom and when?" Keith replied, "from an
honest woman, yet living not far distant." He knew too
much. They asked him, "Art thou not a treacherous
man to tell this?" Keith naively added, "it is a thing
well enough known to themselves that they have collections at their monthly and quarterly meetings, one chief
use whereof is, to furnish the travelling Friends with
money." And thus ended the first attempt to introduce
the Church in Flushing.

However, he was not discouraged. He returned on
the second of December, 1702, less than three months
after his first memorable visit. He had obtained a letter from Lord Cornbury, the Governor of the Province,
directing two justices of the peace to go with him to
protect him from interruption. This was a mere parade
of power, for Keith knew too well the principles of his
former co-religionists to fear any bodily harm. It was
on "First Day," or Sunday morning, and a full congregation would be present, as the Friends in those days
made it a matter of conscience to "attend meeting."
The invaders entered the meeting—Keith and his associ-

ate, Mr. Talbot, and the representatives of the magiste-
rial power, in the Governor's two justices of the peace.
It was the Law and the Gospel. It would seem that
without any preliminaries the visitors began their work.
They broke in upon the "silent meeting," which always
begins as soon as a Friend enters the meeting, whether
he be the first, or whether hundreds have entered before
him. Mr. Talbot produced the Governor's letter to the
justices, authorizing them to prevent the Quakers from
any interruption. It was read to the meeting. We
are prepared to hear Mr. Keith's complaint. "They took
no notice of my Lord Cornbury's letter, more than if it
had been from any private person." Nor were they awed
in the least by the justices, "but," says Keith, "renewed their former interruption." Of course they did,
and that rightly and righteously.

After a stormy meeting most of the Friends left the
meeting-house. Many who were not Quakers remained,
and Keith and his more amiable associate had the meeting to themselves. Some of them, no doubt, were Church
of England men, glad to hear once more the word "spoken
in their own tongue." It would bring to the air and re-
kindle the coals long smouldering and hidden under disuse and the absence of all the forms of religion. It was
to them like the old hearth-stone song of early days, in
a strange land. It revived old memories.

As far as we have documentary evidence thus ended
the last visit of Keith and Talbot to Flushing. Although we must not "make history," we may legiti-
mately refer to the well-known course of Keith and his
associate in their missionary work. They were no mere
itinerant preachers, but workers and builders. Wherever
a possibility existed, the scattered members of the Church
of England were sought out and gathered together, and

some attempt at organization was made. Keith was a
man of rare executive ability, a clever organizer, and
had great power in inspiring men to work. He and
Talbot gathered the nuclei of congregations, and began the work of building churches everywhere. The
venerable Parish of St. Mary's, Burlington, N. J., was
thus begun, and Talbot was long its Rector. In Hempstead and Jamaica the work received a successful impe-
tus. At Oyster Bay, Huntington and elsewhere on
Long Island, a beginning was made. It is no flight of
fancy then, to suppose that a like effort was made in
Flushing, and the few scattered families of Mother Church
were commended to the care of the Rector of Jamaica.
Keith and Talbot began the work in Flushing, and their
visits here are memorable events in the history of St.
George's Church. They at least "staked out" the future
parish, and in faith left the result with God.

We have given all that the records furnish of the visits
of the Rev. George Keith and the Rev. John Talbot to
Flushing. These early pioneers deserve more than a
passing notice. Our old Long Island parishes owe them
a debt of grateful memory.

Mr. Keith had been a member of the Society of Friends
for more than thirty years when he left England for the
Colony of Penn. He came as a Quaker and a propagandist of his sect, and labored with his characteristic zeal.
For a time he was Surveyor-General in "East Jersey,"
but was better known as an eminent public Friend. He
soon discovered among the Friends in the Colonies tendencies to dangerous errors which had not appeared
among the more conservative Quakers in England. The
fundamental doctrines relating to the death and resurrec-
tion of our Lord, and to the reconciliation of man through
Him, were ignored or denied. Quaker though he was,

THE SEAL OF THE SOCIETY FOR THE PROPAGATION OF
GOSPEL.

he held the dogmatic faith as the Friends in England held
it. There was a bitter contention, and soon a clear-cut
schism. In "East Jersey" and other localities "Meetings" were formed of the "Keithians" who claimed to
be the original Friends. It was from these that Keith and
Talbot afterward persuaded so many to return to the
Church of England. After Keith's retirement the schism
seemed to disappear. But the cause of it survived, to
reappear later in the Hicksite controversy, and the final
separation of the Orthodox Friends as a distinct body in
1827.

   In 1700 Keith published his "Reasons for Renouncing
the Sect called Quakers," and became a candidate for
Holy Orders. As soon as he was ordained he was sent
by the Society for the Propagation of the Gospel on his
famous "mission of observation," to discover and study
the state of religion in the Colonies, and report where
missionaries could be sent and missions established. It
was while he was on this important mission that he visited Flushing in 1702.

   Because of his ardent temperament and tireless energy,
Keith's zeal may not always have been tempered with
moderation. He had the fault of his times in a dogmatic
and impatient spirit. Strong in his convictions, bold and
outspoken, he naturally made many enemies. The venerable Society sent out no missionary more self-sacrific-
ing and successful than George Keith. He began the
work and laid the foundations on which others built.

   The early Quakers had in him their strongest and most
learned advocate, and when he left them the Church found
in him a most faithful and competent agent for the work
assigned him.

   John Talbot was a man of different temperament.
Amiable, fluent and eloquent, a scholar and gentleman,

he was not less zealous and successful than his older companion. They worked together as brothers, in love and mutual appreciation, in their "mission of observation" through the Colonies. Keith was the hammer—*malleus haereticorum*—while Talbot with gentler hand, smoothed the way and persuaded men. Talbot may be called the builder of congregations and churches. He founded the parish and built the old Church of St. Mary's, Burlington, and was its first Rector. He ranked as the oldest missionary in the Colonies when he retired, and in his influence he stood first in the Church in East Jersey and Pennsylvania.

But after more than twenty years' successful labor, a cloud settled upon his course, under the deep shadow of which he died. This introduces a startling peril with which the Church in the Colonies was menaced, and a bit of history with its instructive warning. He had long felt the indispensible need of actual supervision of the Colonial Churches by a bishop. No one wrote oftener to the Society on the subject. But it was all in vain. The bishops could not act without the Government, and the Government cared little and did less for the Colonial Church. Talbot despaired of ever seeing a bishop in this country. He seems suddenly to have called to mind the non-juring bishops of England. As is well known, certain bishops of that kingdom had refused to take the oaths to William and Mary, after the revolution of 1688. They were deprived of their sees for their loyalty to the Stuarts, and others were put into their places. Some of them lived for many years, and took pains to keep up the succession by conferring the episcopal authority on others.

Talbot asked the Society for leave to visit England in 1720. Obtaining this, he resolved upon a step always perilous in such cases. It was an appeal to the law of supposed necessity. He determined to obtain the boon of the episcopate, by seeking consecration at the hands of the non-juring bishops. In this case to appeal to necessity was to distrust Providence and to tempt Christ. He was privately consecrated soon after the Rev. Dr. Welton, and the fact was not widely known for years after. He returned after an absence of two years, and quietly resumed his duties in Burlington. It was soon whispered around that he and Dr. Welton were in episcopal orders. Both visited some southern colonies, and there appeared in episcopal robes and confirmed a few persons. So it was reported. Dr. Welton was invited to Christ Church, Philadelphia, and Mr. Talbot continued his labors in Burlington. Neither, it would seem, openly claimed episcopal orders or jurisdiction. But a matter of this nature could not escape suspicion. The clergy were alarmed in all the Colonies. It reached the ears of the civil authority. The Government saw the spectre of an Episcopate in the Colonies independent of Church and State, derived from a source opposed to the reigning house in England, and in hostile separation from the ruling ecclesiastical authority. It was disloyalty in robes and mitre. The Governor of Pennsylvania received an order, enclosing his majesty's writ of privy-seal, commanding Welton, under penalty, to return to Great Britain. Mr. Talbot at the same time was discharged from the employment of the Venerable Society, and was inhibited by the Governor of the Province, by instruction from home, from preaching or performing any ministerial office. Mr. Talbot submissively obeyed, and spent the few remaining years of his life in retirement and poverty in Burlington. The rest is told by a brief notice in the "American Weekly Mercury." Philadelphia, for November 30, 1727: "Yesterday, died at Burlington, the Rev. John Talbot, formerly minister of that place, who was a pious, good man, and much lamented." On a band in the stained glass of a window in the new St. Mary's Church at Burlington, is this inscription in Latin : "In memory of John Talbot, A. M., the founder of this Church, in A. D. 1703."

So ended the attempt to introduce the Episcopate in the Colonies through the non-juring bishops, sixty years before the Rev. Samuel Seabury was consecrated. No one who reads the story of John Talbot's life and work, will doubt that, in receiving consecration in the way he did, he was actuated by the pure desire to advance the best interests of the Church, or will dissent from the judgment of the late Dr. Hawks, "that the Society never had a more honest, fearless and laborious missionary."

CHAPTER III.

IT is difficult to state when Divine service was first regularly held in Flushing by a clergyman of the Church of England. The documentary history of this subject is very limited, and consists rather of incidental notices than of any special record. It is from these that we have to gather our information. During the eighteenth century the history of the Parishes of Flushing and Newtown is blended with that of the Parish of Jamaica. The last named is the oldest parish, and was the residence of the rector. The other two were within his parochial bounds and under his personal ministry. He was duly inducted as Rector of Jamaica by authority of the Governor of the Province. The Venerable Society appointed him as a missionary under their rules and regulations, and Newtown and Flushing were included within his cure.

The first clergyman sent by the Venerable Society was the Rev. Patrick Gordon, who came over as chaplain of an English man-of-war with Keith and Talbot. He landed in June, 1702. He visited the Rev. Dr. Vesey, the Rector of Trinity Church, New York, who was then recovering from an attack of yellow fever. He set out for his parish at Jamaica, designing to preach there and enter upon his work. But he was suddenly stricken with fever and died eight days after. The Rev. Mr. Talbot, in his letter

THE ORIGINAL DEED FOR THE CHURCHYARD.

to the Society, wrote: "Mr. Gordon, Rector of Queens County, to the grief of all good men, is removed by death." This was in June, 1702.

After Mr. Gordon's death, the Rev. Mr. Bartow preached on alternate Sundays in Jamaica, "at his own charge." In 1704, a man whose name well deserves to be commemorated in the Colonial History of the Church, took up the work in Jamaica and its dependencies. He was the Rev. James Honeyman. Lord Cornbury "granted him admission to the ministerial function in Jamaica." He really began the work in the three towns. Earnest, and of the Church-militant order, his effective ministry was soon felt. He raised a veritable tempest around him, in exciting the ire of "the enemies of our religion," whom he "strove to bring over to Christianity." He writes: "To this parish (Jamaica) belong two other towns; viz., Newtown and Flushing; the latter famous for being stocked with Quakers, whither I intend to go, upon their meeting days, on purpose to preach lectures against their errors."

It will be noted that he was not sent by the Venerable Society, but received a license from the Governor at his pleasure and until a rector should be sent. Upon the arrival of Mr. Gordon's successor in 1704, Mr. Honeyman went to Newport, R. I., where he established the Church amid difficulties, which would have appalled any but the bravest heart. He continued there for forty-five years, and ranks with Bartow and Talbot as the founder of parishes.

The Rev. William Urquhart was inducted in July, 1704, as rector. He was the third minister in Jamaica. We find in a letter from the Rev. Mr. Talbot, the following commendation: "Mr. Urquhart is well chosen for the people of Jamaica; and, indeed, I think none fitter than the Scotch

Episcopal to deal with Whigs and fanatics of all sorts."
This is significant and reveals the spirit of the age. The
"dissenters" in Jamaica of that day do not seem to have
been of a very gentle sort. The old prejudice against the
Church burned and glowed, and Lord Cornbury's meth-
ods did not tend to allay the heat. Colonel Heathcote
wrote in 1705 : "Mr. Urquhart, minister in Jamaica, has
the most difficult task of any missionary in this government—having a Presbyterian meeting-house on the one
hand and the Quakers on the other, and very little assistance in his parish, his work can but go on heavily." We
read that he "became the third husband of Mary,
daughter of Daniel Whitehead, by the use of whose
money he became the patentee of a tract of land in New
Jersey."

Mr. Urquhart resided at Jamaica, but Newtown and Flushing were under his pastoral charge. He held service and
preached twice on two successive Sundays in Jamaica, on
the third Sunday he read service and preached twice at
Newtown, and "at Flushing once a month on the week
days." In his report he says : "By the blessing of God
the congregations in the respective towns daily increase."
There was no church building or "meeting-house," built
by a tax on the people, in Flushing as in the other towns.
The guard house or, as afterward called, the town house,
was the only building in which a congregation could be
called together. Here the Church services were held.
The Guard House stood "west of the pond," near where
the fountain now stands in the village park. It was
erected in the early days of Flushing, for refuge and de-
fence, and was afterward used for a town hall.

Mr. Urquhart evidently was not very enthusiastic about
his work in Flushing, but it is evident he held stated services here. No record of such services exists, but the simple

fact is stated and that the congregation increased. But whatever his success or discouragement, the fact is established that as early as 1704 stated services were held in Flushing, and that for many years the old Guard House was the place where the faithful were accustomed to meet for public worship.

Mr. Urquhart died in 1709. We have not spoken of his controversy with the dissenters concerning his right to the church and glebe. This parish (Flushing) was only indirectly affected by the controversy. It belongs rather to the history of Grace Church, Jamaica. We may say in passing that in that early period of our history, the particular names by which the parishes are now known do not appear, such as Grace Church, Jamaica; St. James' Church, Newtown, or St. George's, Flushing. The name of our parish does not occur in our charter, 1761. It is simply "The Inhabitants of the Town of Flushing, in Communion of the Church of England." Strictly speaking, the name of St. George belongs to the parish church, as erected to the glory of God, and in memory of St. George.

CHAPTER IV.

THE Rev. Mr. Urquhart was succeeded by the Rev.
Thomas Poyer in 1710. This good man and faithful minister did the work of an evangelist with almost
apostolical self-denial and labor.

Mr. Poyer was born in Wales. He was the grandson of
Colonel Poyer, the heroic defender of Pembroke Castle
during Cromwell's time. Mr. Poyer was brought up
in a refined family, and was educated at Oxford. In
1706 he was ordained deacon by Bishop Lloyd, and
three months after he was ordained priest by the celebrated Dr. Bull, the Bishop of St. David's. His first field
of labor was at Burton in Pembrokeshire.

Three years later, December 16th, 1709, he offered his
services to the Society for the Propagation of the Gospel,
and was appointed Missionary to Jamaica, Flushing and
Newtown. The Bishop of London granted him license,
and on the 30th day of the same month, December, 1709,
he embarked for America. After a voyage of more than
three months, his ship was wrecked on the coast of Long
Island, a hundred miles from his parish. When he reached
Jamaica he found that the parsonage was in the possession of the dissenters. His predecessor's widow had delivered it to them the day before his expected arrival.
Suspiciously enough Mrs. Urquhart was readmitted to the
parsonage shortly afterward.

But, nothing daunted, Mr. Poyer began his work. He

had inherited his grandfather's courage and, perhaps, a trifle of his pugnacity.   With a frequent exchange of suits of ejectment between him and the dissenters, he bravely began his work as missionary to the three parishes.   His predecessor found the Quaker element in Flushing too

SAMPLER, WITH A SKETCH OF THE FIRST CHURCH.

hard for him—it turned the edge of his sword.   Mr. Urquhart had described Newtown as "a place well affected, desirous to have a minister;" but Flushing, he said, was a town of Quakers, "who rove through the country and talk blasphemy, corrupt the youth, and do much mischief."

In his report to the Society, dated, May 3, 1711, Mr.
Poyer says: "I thank God the Church of England in-
creaseth, for among the Quakers at Flushing, where Mr.
Urquhart, in all the time of his mission, could never
gather a congregation, I have seldom so few as fifty hearers. I have great hopes that more will come over to our
Church, notwithstanding the many enemies and discour-
agements I meet withal." Again, in 1713, he writes:
"The churches increase beyond expectation; and among
the Quakers in Flushing (where Mr. Urquhart did not
think it worth while to go) I seldom have so few as fifty
and often more than an hundred hearers."

Mr. Poyer was a man of boots as well as of books and
"preachments." The Society had furnished him with
good books adapted to the needs and errors of the times.
As he went about in his parishes he loaned or gave these
books to persons who would read them, and thus he educated the people in the doctrines of the Church. He
also sought out the children and gathered them together
for Catechetical instruction.

We cannot give many details of Mr. Poyer's pastoral
work in Flushing. His custom was to give frequent lectures on week days; and to instruct in the Catechism all
such as were sent to him, twice a week in the church,
and once a fortnight the year round at his house. It does
not appear how much Flushing and Newtown were ben-
efited by these abundant labors. There is no doubt they
had their full share. This, some incidental remarks in
his reports make evident. He speaks of his parish as fifteen miles long and more than six broad, and says that
this compelled him to keep two horses, which he "found
expensive and troublesome." He complains that so much
riding wore out more clothes in a year than would be
needed in three or four years if he had not to ride Evi-

dently Flushing had its full share of his labors. He went from house to house over the then rough and sparsely settled country. The people were pioneers, often rude and indifferent to religion, or bitter in their prejudices. He had few to encourage or welcome him. He writes : "In Flushing and Newtown there is no convenience of private houses, so I have to use public houses at very great charge, for I usually bring some of my family with me."

Much has been said and written to the detriment of the Colonial clergy. It must be admitted that in two of the southern colonies, where the Church was established by law, many did not live answerably to their holy calling. But it was far otherwise in the northern colonies, where there was little in the Church to attract unworthy men. The clergy had no establishment to lure or shield them. In endurance, as good soldiers of Christ, in self-sacrifice, in earnest work in the face of poverty, persecution and relentless opposition, the clergymen in these northern colonies compare favorably with those in ancient or modern days.

Mr. Poyer proved his noble disinterestedness. He received £50 a year from the Society and very little from any other source. He declined a call to the West Indies with a salary of £400, because he feared Jamaica. Newtown and Flushing would be left without a clergyman. His parish was no worldly paradise. As a Church clergyman he had to feel the enmity which then burned against the Church. He put up with affronts and abuse. He wrote to the Society in 1718 : "They tried to tire me out with ill-usage." The shop-keepers would not sell him provisions. The dissenting miller sent back his grain unground, with the message to eat it whole as his hogs did. Oppressed by debts he could not avoid—the

devil's gridiron on which poor parsons are roasted—he
found himself, at times, under the bailiff's tender surveil-
lance. At length the brave heart failed. In 1731, he
complained to the Society that the infirmities of old age
were bearing hard upon him. With pathetic appeal he
asked permission to leave his work and return to his native land. It was man's last and universal instinct : "Let
me return to my kindred and be buried with my fathers."
His request was granted, but he never returned. In December of that year he was stricken with small-pox, then
epidemic in Jamaica. It was half a century before Jen-
ner's discovery of vaccination. He died on the last day
of the year, 1731, and was buried in the village cemetery.
No stone marks his grave. He rests in peace.

Thus died a worthy man. He had labored in the parish
for more than twenty-three years, and deserves of St.
George's parish the tribute of a lasting and grateful
memory.

A frequent cause of Mr. Poyer's litigations in Jamaica
was the non-payment of the salary voted by the town.
This amounted to about $150, and was raised by a tax
upon the ratable inhabitants. By an act of the Colonial
Assembly as early as 1693, a law was passed, called "the
Minister's Act," for the settlement of a minister, and raising a maintenance, in the counties of New York, Westchester, Richmond and Queens. "A good and sufficient
Protestant minister" was to be called and inducted to
officiate and have the cure of souls ; and a tax for his
support was to be assessed upon the free-holders, without
reference to religious creed or profession. In 1695, the
House of Assembly enlarged this act by providing that
two church wardens and ten vestrymen should be elected
annually by all the freeholders. It was to be the duty of
the wardens and vestrymen, together with the justices,

to fix the rate of the tax, and the amount to be paid to the minister. They were to see that the tax was levied and that the minister received his salary.

In those days the tax could be paid *in kind*, that is, in grain or other commodity. The law required the vestry to receive and sell this and pay the minister. As the wardens and vestrymen were elected by all the freeholders who were largely "dissenters," dissenting vestries were often chosen. On this account Mr. Poyer was often obliged to compel them by suits at law to levy the tax, then by mandamuses to sell the grain, and then again to appeal to the courts to enforce the payment of his salary. This was a mode of support worse even than the now happily obsolete "donation parties," and gave the poor parson's adversaries another way "to tire him out."

But in this they failed. Mr. Poyer held on and, what was a greater grievance, still "held the fort" in occupying the "old square meeting-house in the middle of the highway." At length the "patience of the saints" was fairly worn out. The dissenting brethren took possession of the meeting-house *vi et armis*. An ejectment suit followed, and Mr. Poyer was defeated, and left without a place of worship. This decision was a great blessing in disguise to the parish of Jamaica. Mr. Poyer removed his congregation to the "town house," where they worshipped for several years (1727—1734), like the congregation in Flushing, "in their own hired house." This was the termination of a controversy which for twenty-five years had disturbed the peace of the Church in Jamaica, and had affected the work even in Flushing.

CHAPTER V.

THE Rev. Thomas Colgan was chosen to succeed Mr. Poyer. He was inducted as rector in January, 1733. He had been an assistant in Trinity Church, New York, and was highly commended by the Rector, Dr. Vesey, and by the wardens of that parish. He had been very successful there as Catechist among the negro population, and had quite a reputation as a reader and preacher. He had officiated in Jamaica since June, 1732, and consequently knew his wide field of labor. His amiable wife was a niece of Mrs. Vesey, and a daughter of Mr. John Reade. Her patrimony, with his own force of character, soon procured for him a better social position than had been enjoyed by his persecuted predecessor.

The congregations under the charge of Mr. Colgan soon began to increase. His prudent and conciliatory course mollified the opposition to the Church. A congregation of more than 200 came to the services at Jamaica, and "joined in the worship with decency and devotion." In Newtown and Flushing there was a similar encouraging change.

Grace Church, Jamaica, was built during Mr. Colgan's rectorship of the united parishes. The first service was held in the new church on Friday, April 5, 1734. Governor Crosby was present, and the whole town turned out, militia and people, to do honor to the joyful occasion.

Mr. Colgan soon began to report progress in all his

congregations. In 1736, he informed the Venerable Society that the Independents, who formerly thought it
almost a crime to join with Churchmen in worship, now
freely came to church and "joined with seeming sanctity
and satisfaction in our service." Later, he reported that
in Flushing, as well as elsewhere, the Church was "in a
growing condition, and never in as flourishing a state as
at present." The spirit that aroused the good people of
Jamaica to build a church, extended to Flushing. In
1746, Mr. Colgan wrote to the Society: "We are likely

WOODEN MODEL OF FIRST CHURCH MADE IN THE EARLY PART OF
THIS CENTURY.

to have a church erected in Flushing, a place generally
inhabited by Quakers, and some of no religion at all."
He expresses the hope that it would be ready for service
in three months, and asks that the Society "bestow a
Bible and Common Prayer Book according to its usual
bounty, for certainly there can be no set of people within
this Province who are greater objects of the Society's pity
and charity than those belonging to the town of Flush-

ing, of which I have been so truly sensible that it has brought me (if I may be permitted thus to express it) to double my diligence in that place where error and impiety greatly abound." This request was granted and the Bible and Prayer Book came in due time, but the precise date cannot be deciphered. The Prayer Book and Bible are bound up together with "The Whole Book of Psalms Collected into English Metre: By Thomas Sternhold and John Hopkins." This book is still in the parish archives. On the page of the "Table of Contents" of the Prayer Book is an engraved imprint of the seal of the Society, with a scroll on which is engraved: "The gift of the Society for the Propagation of the Gospel in Foreign Parts" Under the engraving is written in a bold hand, "To the Church in Flushing," with a date partly mutilated, but which seems to be, 1754. The book (page 14) has been rebound and the figures were cut off by the binder.

After occupying "the Block House near the pond," as a place of worship for forty years, the struggling congregation in Flushing had a habitation as well as a name. In the absence of official records, we glean what we can from fragmentary notices. From these we learn that the church building owed its origin mainly to the efforts of one man. As already stated, Mr. Colgan wrote to the Society in 1745: "We are likely to have a church in Flushing." He stated further that "the church was almost finished by the means and bounty in a good measure, of the worthy Captain Hugh Wentworth, who had given the grounds for the church and churchyard, and by a great pecuniary subscription contributed largely to the building itself." Captain Wentworth was a merchant in the West Indian trade, and owned a tract of land in Flushing. It was a farm lying on the highway to Jamaica, and extending southerly from the present corner of Lincoln and Main streets. The plot he gave is the site now occupied by the church and churchyard.

The original deed is in the possession of the Vestry. It was found among Mr. Colgan's papers, mutilated by rats. The land was given by Hugh Wentworth and Mary, his wife, " for the encouragement of building a church in Flushing and other good causes." The property is described as " all that certain small spot of land in the Town of Flushing bounded easterly by the highway leading from Flushing to Jamaica, and northerly by the widow Hinchman, and southerly and westerly by the other land of the said Hugh Wentworth, containing the full and exact quantity of half an acre of land, for the sole use and behoof * * * of the church erected and on the spot of land now standing * * * conveniency of a church yard, and to and for no other use or uses whatsoever from henceforth forevermore." The deed is signed by Hugh Wentworth and Mary Wentworth, and was " sealed and delivered in presence of John Groesbeck, James Lyon, John Burgess."

The deed is dated, April 7, 1749. It was given consequently, some years after the completion of the church. The church was finished and first used for worship in 1746. We may assume that, in accordance with universal usage, the name of St. George was, at that time, given it.

Three years later, in 1749, Mr. Colgan writes that, " a Quaker gave some money at the opening of the new church and afterward thought he had not put enough in the plate and gave more to the collector." Though nameless, his good deed is recorded as an example worthy of imitation. This is the only incident recorded in connection with the opening of the new church.

We know little about the appearance of the first Church. The only picture of it now existing is the

contemporary sketch on a "sampler." Two such sam-
plers are in existence in Flushing, each having a similar
picture of a church, which trustworthy tradition says
was sketched from the first St. George's Church. There
is also preserved in the church to-day a small wooden
model of the first church, made by a boy, in the early
part of the century. The spire has been lost and the
position of the tower is not the same as in the sketch.
The writing of a wag on the door of the Flushing church,
described it as "a little church and a high steeple." The
witticism was founded on fact.

A spire, or steeple, was considered almost an essential
to a church belonging to the Church of England in those
days. It distinguished it as such. "The steeple house"
was the common name given to a church by the Puri-
tans. But the spire or steeple, was not at first built.
The Church stood about ten years without it

Mr. Colgan died in December, 1755, "lamented and
respected by all who knew him," after a ministry of more
than twenty-three years in the united parishes. Three
churches were built during his rectorship; viz., at
Jamaica, Newtown, and Flushing. He found the
churches in a depressed state, but from no fault of his
persecuted and enduring predecessor. The tide had
reached its ebb when he came. In his second year he
reported encouraging progress. He wrote at the same
time: "We are at peace with the sectaries that are
round about us, and I hope that by God's help, peace
will subsist among us. To sow the seeds thereof shall
be my endeavor ; to be of a loving, charitable demeanor
to all, of whatever persuasion in matters of religion,
shall be, by God's help, my practice, that so discharging
my duties herein, I may contribute my mite to the good
of the Church of Christ." Unwittingly, Mr. Colgan in

this, drew the portrait of his ministry. We are ready to exclaim. "*O si sic omnes!*" The result of his labors shows us his Christian spirit. His prudent bearing did much to soften the asperities of the sects among themselves, to allay prejudice against the Church, and to gain the good will of all.

CHAPTER VI.

A GREAT danger threatened the united parishes of
Jamaica, Newtown and Flushing after the death of
Mr. Colgan.

The dissenters had a majority in the vestry at Jamaica
and the old feud between them and the Churchmen revived. They made choice of a Presbyterian minister
to succeed Mr. Colgan, and presented his name to Governor Hardy for induction. This action, if successful,
would have been destructive to the struggling parishes,
and would have left them without the service of the
Church. But Governor Hardy, "in obedience to instructions from his Majesty," could not admit the minister
presented because he could not procure a certificate under
seal from the Bishop of London, of conformity to the
Church of England. The vestry would present no one
else. So the matter stood. After waiting half a year, Governor Hardy took matters into his own hands, and "his
Excellency was pleased to collate to the cure of the parish,
the Rev. Samuel Seabury, Jr., in 1755." He afterwards
became the first bishop of the Protestant Episcopal
Church. During Mr. Seabury's rectorship, Mr. John Aspinwall, a retired merchant, removed from New York to

Flushing. He is described in a letter of the time, as "a zealous Churchman, and a man of great public spirit and large fortune." The presence of an earnest, energetic, open-hearted Christian layman, of enlarged views, was a new and disturbing element in the sluggish life of a rural community.

From Perry's History.
THE RT. REV. SAMUEL SEABURY, D. D.

Mr. Aspinwall's residence still stands as one of the landmarks of older Flushing. It was long known as the "Bloodgood mansion," and is now the residence of Mr. Paul De Lacy Lieberman. Associated in Mr. Aspinwall's good work was Mr. Thomas Grenell, a loyal and active Churchman, whose name is worthy of a place among the

zealous workers of St. George's Church. Mr. Aspinwall
did not find the religious state of Flushing to correspond
with its advantages and beauty of location. A contemporary, in a letter still extant, gives a gloomy picture.
He writes : "Mr. Aspinwall found the inhabitants almost
devoid of all sense of religion, with a total dissolution of
all manners, and a horrid contempt of the Sabbath."
Fain would we tone down this rugged picture. But the
reports of Mr. Seabury to the Society, confirm the state-
ment. In 1759 he wrote this pregnant sentence : "Flushing, in the last generation the grand seat of Quakerism,
is in this, the seat of Deism and infidelity. Bred up in
entire neglect of all forms in worship, in contempt of the
ministry and sacraments, and the practical denial of the
need of any redemption, it seems a natural transition,
and hard is their conversion ! Even among the members
of the Church there is a great backwardness in attending
her services and sacraments, growing out of the prevail-
ing religious indifference." * * * "Preaching once
in three weeks at a place, I find by experience, will do
little more than keep up the present languid sense of
religion, and were it not for the steady though slow increase in Newtown I should be quite discouraged."

Mr. Aspinwall speedily attempted a reformation. His
first step seems like a prophetical one. He established a
school. This was the beginning of Flushing schools.
He induced Mr. Treadwell, of New York, to settle in
Flushing and establish a Latin school. His next step
was to finish the church, and provide the decent appointments of public worship. The letter quoted above, says:
"He found the church an unfinished shell." His first
move was to finish it, and make it comfortable and attractive. The good people had grace enough, and sense
enough, to let him take the lead. He finished and fur-

nished the interior, and "built a handsome steeple, and gave a very fine bell." All this was "at his own cost amounting to £600." "It is now," adds the enthusiastic writer, "one of the neatest churches of its bigness in America." The vane on the present chapel is the same one placed on the completed church at that time. This was in A. D., 1760.

The bell of the first church had on it the inscription : "The gift of John Aspinwall, Gentleman, 1760." It weighed about 400 pounds. When, in 1853, the present church was building and a larger bell was required, Mr. William H. Aspinwall, and his brother John, generously claimed the right to give the new bell, on condition that the old one should be recast in the new. This was carefully complied with. The old bell was taken to the Troy foundry, broken up and put into the melting pot in the presence of a member of the vestry, appointed for that purpose,—the late W. H. Schermerhorn, Esq. The old inscription was cast on the new bell, with an appropriate addition of the names and date of gift of the original donor's descendants.

Before the advent of Mr. Aspinwall, service had been held but once in three weeks, in Flushing, roads and weather permitting. Mr. Aspinwall induced Mr. Tread-well to become a lay reader, and hold a service every Sunday. The effect of this was soon visible. In the letter from which we have quoted, it is said : "He (Mr. A.) and Mr. Treadwell by their own good ex-ample and pious labors, brought together a numerous congregation, where for the last four years seldom more than ten persons assembled. Such has been the happy effect of example." And such we may add, were the happy results of lay work in the early days of the parish.

Mr. Seabury, during his earnest pastorate, moved to obtain a charter for each of the three parishes. We judge that its inception was his because the petitions for the charters were similar, and made in the same year. The petition from Flushing, dated the 27th of May, 1761, was made to the Hon. Cadwallader Colden, President of the Council of the Province of New York. It set forth that the petitioners and the rest of the inhabitants of the town of Flushing, in communion of the Church of England by law established, had long labored under great inconvenience because of the lack of regular Divine service, and had found it very discouraging to the cause of religion ; that they had at great expense erected a decent place of worship in the name of St. George's Church, and obtained half an acre of land adjoining for the use of a cemetery, and had determined to make suitable provision for the support of a minister to be called to the care of the church ; but that the petitioners and the rest of the inhabitants of Flushing could not carry on the good design without being incorporated, so as to receive donations and dispose of the same. Therefore they asked for Letters Patent to create them a body politic and corporate.

This petition was signed by twenty-one persons. The petition from Jamaica, sent ten days earlier, had twenty-four signatures : that of Newtown, sent four months later, had thirty-four. These lists show the names of the old Church families in the respective parishes, at that date. We subjoin those from Flushing :

John Aspinwall, Thomas Grenell, Daniel Thorne, Joseph Bowne, Joseph Haviland, Jacob Thorne, Francis Brown, Foster Lewis, William Thorne, Charles Cornell, John Morrell, Benjamin Thorne, John Dyer, Jeremiah Mitchell, Nathaniel Tom, Benjamin Fowler, John Marston, Charles Wright, Isaac Doughty, Christopher Robert, John Wilson.

Few of these venerable names are now found among us. They represented families scattered over the large town of Flushing. The vestry appointed by the charter, had for Church Wardens, John Aspinwall and Thomas Grenell ; for Vestrymen, John Dyer, Christopher Robert,

From Perry's History.
SITE OF BISHOP SKINNER'S CHAPEL, ABERDEEN.

John Morrell, Joseph Haviland, Francis Brown and Jeremiah Mitchell, to serve until their successors were chosen, which would be on Easter Tuesday, 1762. The charter is dated June 17, 1761—the first year of George the Third—and St. George's Church took its place among the few incorporated parishes in the Province of New York.

During Mr. Seabury's rectorship, Flushing and Newtown became dissatisfied because they had but one
service in three weeks, and resolved to make better
provision for themselves. After consultation, they asked
the Society's permission to separate from Jamaica and
to be united under the care of one clergyman. As the
two parishes, unaided, could not support a minister, they
applied for an appropriation. They asked that Mr.
Treadwell, the school-master and lay-reader, might go to
England for Holy Orders, and return as their missionary.
Jamaica consented to the arrangement. Mr. Treadwell
went abroad and was ordained. On his return he was to
continue his school in Flushing, "as the nursery of our
infant college"—King's, now Columbia, College. He
returned, but not to live in Flushing. The Society was
moved to decline the appropriation asked for. Mr.
Treadwell was sent by the Bishop of London as missionary to Trenton, N. J. A letter to the Society from
Mr. Seabury may explain this. He speaks of the unquiet
of the Church in Flushing, and complains of Mr. Treadwell's intrusion in holding a service and administering
baptism there, after his return. He says: "All this
was done through one Mr. Aspinwall, who wants Newtown and Flushing set off from Jamaica and to be under
the care of Mr. Treadwell; but the growing expenses of
an increasing family will not permit me to relinquish any
part of my salary." He received twenty pounds from
each of the two parishes.

The former friendly relations between Mr. Seabury and
Mr. Aspinwall became strained, and the harmony between the parishes was broken. Perhaps it was the sign
of life. A peace was temporarily made, but it has been
well said that a Church's dissention is the devil's seed-
time. The reaping soon came. In their disputes, the

parishes forgot their promises to their overworked Rector, and made no provisions for his salary.   The climax
came at length : Mr. Seabury, in 1765, asked to be re-
lieved of his restless charge, and removed to Westchester.

The resignation of Mr. Seabury was a great loss to the
three united parishes.   Their neglect of him during his
rectorship was not because of any dissatisfaction with
him, but because of their mutual jealousy.   Each feared
the others were not bearing their proper share of the general expense, and Newtown and Flushing seemed united
against Jamaica in the feeling that the latter received
more than its due share of the rector's time and attention.

During the disputes with England, which resulted in
the War of Independence, Mr. Seabury—who had taken
an oath of allegiance to the Crown—felt constrained to
take the side of the mother country.   He was seized at
his Westchester home by a band of soldiers and taken a
prisoner to Connecticut.   After regaining his freedom he
supported himself by his skill as a physician—having
studied medicine when a young man at Edinburgh—and
exercised his sacred functions as a priest whenever op-
portunity offered.   At the close of the war, March 25,
1783, he was elected Bishop of Connecticut.   On Sunday,
November 14th, of the following year, he was consecrated in the private chapel of Bishop Skinner, in Aberdeen, by three "non-juring" bishops of Scotland.   He
returned in 1785, the first bishop of the American Church.
In addition to his duties as Bishop of Connecticut, he undertook the rectorship of the parish of New London.
Bishop Seabury died on February 25, 1796.

CHAPTER VII.

THE charter is dated June 17, 1761—the first year of the reign of King George III. It is quite a lengthy document, written on parchment. To it is attached the great seal of the Province of New York. It is drawn up with great care : the duties by it prescribed and the privileges granted are all accurately defined. So wise and judicious did its provisions appear that the parish of St. Peter's, Westchester, a year after, petitioned for a charter " with such rights, privileges and immunities as were heretofore granted to the inhabitants of Flushing."

We shall not attempt to give more than an outline of the most important provisions of the charter. It begins thus :

"George the Third, by the Grace of God, of Great Britain, France and Ireland, King, Defender of the Faith, etc., to all to whom these presents shall come, Greeting : Whereas, our loving subjects, John Aspinwall, Thomas Grenell, Daniel Thorne, Joseph Bowne, Joseph Haviland, Jacob Thorne, Francis Brown, Foster Lewis, William Thorne, Charles Cornell, John Morell, Benjamin Thorne, John Dyer, Jeremiah Mitchell, Nathaniel Tom, Benjamin Fowler, John Marston, Charles Wright, Isaac Doughty, Christopher Robert, John Wilson, by their humble petition in behalf of themselves and the rest of the inhabitants of the Township of Flushing, in communion of the Church of England, by law established, presented to our

trusty and well beloved Cadwallader Colden, Esq., President of our Council and Commander-in-Chief of our Province of New York and the territories depending thereon
in America, in council assembled on the 27th day of May,
last past [1761], did set forth that they and the rest of
the inhabitants of Flushing, in communion of the Church
of England," [here follows the petition.] "Which petition having been then and there read and considered of,
our said Council did afterwards on the same day humbly
advise our said President to grant the prayer thereof:
Wherefore, we being willing to give all our encouragement to the pious intentions of our said subjects, and to
grant their reasonable request, Know ye, that we of our
special grace, certain knowledge and mere motion have
made, ordained, constituted, granted and declared, and
by these presents for us and our heirs and successors, do
make, ordain, constitute, grant and declare that the said
petitioners and the rest of the inhabitants of the Town of
Flushing, in communion of the Church of England, and
they and their successors for the time being, by the name
of The Inhabitants of the Township of Flushing, in
Queens County, in communion of the Church of England,
as by law established, one body politick and corporate
in deed, fact and name, really and fully, we do for us,
our heirs and successors erect, make, constitute, declare
and create, by these presents bind that by the same name
they and their successors shall and may have perpetual
succession, etc., as fully as any other corporation within
that part of Great Britain called England."

After granting all the powers and rights of a body corporate, it is provided that "for the better ordering and
managing the affairs and business of the said corporation,
there shall be one minister of the Church of England,
duly qualified for the cure of souls, two church wardens

and six vestrymen elected and chosen for said church as hereafter expressed, which minister and church wardens, or any two of them, with the vestrymen, or major part of them, shall have and are hereby invested with full power and authority to dispose, order and govern the general business affairs of the said church".... "and to have a common seal to serve and use in all matters,".... "And for the better execution of our royal will and pleasure herein, we do assign, constitute and appoint the said John Aspinwall and Thomas Grenell to be the present church wardens, and the said John Dyer, Christopher Robert, John Morell, Joseph Haviland, Francis Brown and Jeremiah Mitchell to be the present vestrymen. And further our will and pleasure is, and we do establish, appoint and direct that the said Tuesday in Easter week next ensuing and once every year thereafter forever on Tuesday in Easter week at the said church, the inhabitants of the Town of Flushing, in communion of the Church of England, or the major part of them, then and there assembled, shall elect, choose and appoint two of their numbers to be church wardens, and six other members to be vestrymen of said church for the year ensuing or until fit persons shall be elected in their respective places."

Another part of the charter relates to the calling of a minister. "And further, for us and our heirs and successors, we do declare and grant that the patronage, advowson, donation or presentation of and to the said church shall appertain and belong to, and is hereby invested in the church wardens and vestrymen for the time being, and their successors forever, or the major part of them whereof one church warden shall always be one."

The original corporate title of the parish was: "The Inhabitants of the Town of Flushing in Communion of

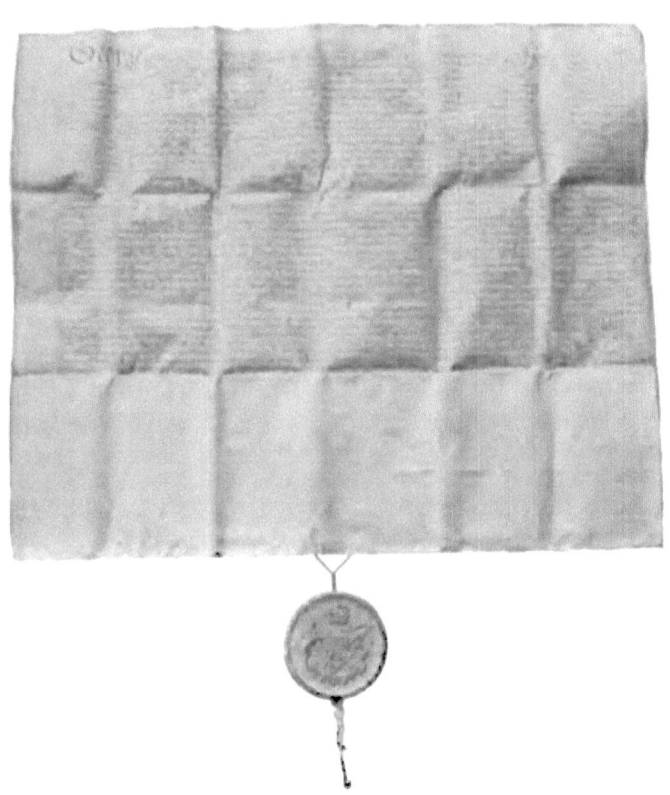

THE PARISH CHARTER A. D. 1701.

the Church of England as by Law Established." Nothing is said about a rector. The Rector of the three parishes resided at Jamaica and received his title from that parish.

When the Legislature of New York revised the Church charters of the State, in 1793, it changed the official title of the parish of Flushing from "The Inhabitants of the Town of Flushing in Communion of the Church of England as by Law Established," to "The Rector and Inhabitants of the Town of Flushing in Communion of the Protestant Episcopal Church in the State of New York." The same act also changed the title Minister, to Rector, and gave him all the rights, privileges and powers of other rectors of the Church in the State of New York, and, as a consequence, gave to the vestry the power to call a rector.

It may be of interest to inquire, how far this charter was affected by the War of Independence, which changed the Province of New York into an independent State. The first Constitution of the State of New York provided that the acts and laws of the colony up to 1775, should be the law of the state, as far as they were not repugnant to the Constitution. This was in 1777. Some of these laws were construed to imply an establishment of the Church of England, as the religion of the Province. The Constitution met this difficulty by ordaining as the organic law of the State, that "the free exercise and enjoyment of religious profession and worship without discrimination or preference shall forever be allowed," and that all acts and laws of the colony "which may be construed to establish or maintain any particular denomination of Christians or their ministers, are repugnant to this Constitution, and are hereby abrogated and rejected." The Legislature, in 1784, enacted, that "to remove all doubts as to the continuance, force and effect of certain acts of legislation of this State as a Colony, passed in 1693" [and enumerating every similar act, to that of 1745], "which do grant certain privileges to the Episcopal Church, or that mode of worship commonly called the Church of England, and which also declare or imply a preference of said Episcopal Church over all other churches, are hereby abrogated, abolished, rescinded and made void."

But when the constitution made the equality of all religious denominations to be the fundamental law of the state, with equal justice it protected all charters and chartered rights granted to churches. It ordained "that nothing in this constitution shall be construed to affect any grant made by the king or his predecessors, or to annul any charters to bodies politic made by him or them prior to October 14, 1775." The charter of St. George's Church was thus recognized and protected by the first Constitution of the State, and has since remained unchanged by any statute of the Legislature, except in a technical enlargement of its corporate title. It is to-day therefore, as operative as it was in June, 1761, unaffected by civil and political changes in the State. The canon of the Diocese of Long Island, "On Parish Boundaries," declares : "The parish boundaries, as defined by the Laws of the State of New York, of the four parishes of St. George's, Flushing, Grace, Jamaica, St. James', Newtown and St. George's, Hempstead, are limited and established by the terms of their several charters." Article L. Canon 2, Section 1.

The question frequently arises, what are the qualifications of a voter at our parish elections. We give the summary of a learned and exhaustive opinion of the late Judge Murray Hoffman : (1) The voters are corporators, and as primary to every qualification, must be " in communion of the Protestant Episcopal Church." "In communion of," is not, "communicants of," but implies a recognition of the doctrines and discipline of the Church, and conformity to its liturgy and worship. (2) They must be "members," that is, corporators, at the time of voting. The charter requires that "they,"— the corporators—"shall meet and choose from their members." None but a corporator can be a church warden or vestryman. The voter must be an "inhabitant" of the Town of Flushing. A non-resident has no vote. (3) A minor can not be a corporator in law, and therefore is not qualified to vote. (4) No vote can be given by proxy. The person voting must be present and offer his vote. The terms of the charter are: "They shall assemble in their church and choose." (5) No one not conforming to the liturgy and worship of the Church, although he may hire or own a pew, is entitled to vote, because such conformity is the ground upon which the charter was granted, and is the obligation assumed by the corporators. (6) A woman can not be a corporator in general. At the date of the charter, it was not competent for women to vote in common law. In the absence of any express provision in a charter, or act of incorporation conferring the right, it is held that women are not legally qualified. Under the statutes of the state, only "males of full age" can vote at church elections.

Another question has sometimes arisen in the election of a vestry under the charter. Occasionally there has been a failure by the corporators to elect a full board. A majority of all the votes is required. But no provision is made by the charter to remedy such failure. In case of death or resignation, "the rector, together with the church wardens or any two of them may" call an election within twenty days. It was maintained that, since the

charter made no provision for such a failure, the old
board should continue in office—their term of office, as
provided by the charter, being "until their successors
shall be chose." This at first was Judge Hoffman's opinion. Subsequently, however, he rendered the following
opinion : "As to failure to elect, the case of the Union
Insurance Co. (22 Wend. pp. 592-600) has caused me to
modify my views to this extent—that if four or five vestrymen are elected—a working majority—and failure as
to one or two, the elected members are entitled to their
seats, and a new election called to fill the vacancy or va-
cancies under the provisions of the charter as to how va-
cancies arising from death or resignation shall be filled."
This reasonable opinion has been followed since it was
kindly given. The failure to elect "a working majority"
has never occurred, and remains an open question which,
it is hoped, may not often require an answer.

CHAPTER VIII.

AFTER the departure of the Rev. Mr. Seabury, the
parishes were for three years without a rector.
The Society refused to continue its annual appropriation
of £40, because the parishes had failed to fulfil their obligations to Mr. Seabury. They finally appealed to Dr.
Auchmuty, Rector of Trinity Church, New York, to come
to their assistance. He called the three congregations
together, preached an earnest sermon on the evils of di-
vision and urged them to live in peace and harmony.
He then heard the different accounts of their grievances,
and finally undertook to persuade the Society to renew
its contributions for their support. His efforts in this direction were successful. The Society recommended Mr.
Joshua Bloomer to the Bishop of London for Holy Orders
and appointed him "Missionary at Jamaica, Newtown
and Flushing." The Secretary of the Society wrote to
Dr. Auchmuty: "It had been determined not to send
another missionary to those places on account of the
great deficiency of the people in making good their promised contributions to their late minister, Mr. Seabury.
But your and Mr. Inglis' kind interposition in their behalf, have induced the Society to depart from their former

resolution. I have directed the people of Jamaica, New-town and Flushing to deliver their obligations for their promised contributions in favour of Mr. Bloomer into your hands." This letter bears date February 28, 1769—the day of Mr. Bloomer's ordination.

The Society was to pay the missionary £20 per annum. Each of the three congregations pledged itself to contribute £30 per annum for his support. A subscription paper was started in Flushing and bears the signatures of thirty-one persons who pledged themselves in sums from two shillings to £3 per annum. The paper was dated, May 23, 1769, the day appointed by the Governor, Sir Henry Moore, for the induction of the new rector.

The Induction Service was very impressive. According to its rule, the church was closed, the ponderous key left in the door, and the people were standing around in the church-yard. The minister came, accompanied by the vestries, and stood before the closed door. The inducting person, a clergyman, or perhaps a church warden, stood at his side with the Governor's warrant of Induction. He then took the minister's right hand and placed it on the key, and pronounced the words: "By virtue of this warrant I induct you, Joshua Bloomer, into the real, actual and corporal possession of the parish church of Jamaica, called Grace Church, including the parish churches of Newtown and Flushing, with all their rights, members and appurtenances." The warden then opened the door and "put the minister in possession thereof," and henceforth the church was his for all sacred services and uses. The minister then tolled the bell and entered the church, followed by the people. The Common Prayer was said, and after its close the minister solemnly declared his assent to all contained therein. The

people then saluted and welcomed their minister and
bade him God speed.   Henceforth he was theirs and they
were his.

The Rev. Joshua Bloomer was born in Westchester
County, in 1735.   He entered King's (now Columbia)
College, and was graduated, with the degree of M. A. in

STAMP ON THE COVER OF THE VESTRY BOOK.

1758.   His was the first class that graduated from the
college.   Among his fellow graduates, were Samuel Provoost, afterward the first Bishop of New York, Chancellor
Joseph Reade, Judge Isaac Ogden, and others whose
names are prominent in colonial history.   Mr. Bloomer

chose the military profession, and in 1759 entered the
service as captain in the provincial forces raised in his
native county, for operations against the French in Canada. He was soon promoted, and served with distinc-
tion as major in the expedition of 1760. After the war
he returned and entered mercantile life in New York. In
this undertaking he was not successful. Later he resolved
to follow out an earlier conviction and devote himself
to the work of the ministry in the Church. He went to
England to prepare for Holy Orders and to offer himself
to the Society as a missionary to his native land, whose
spiritual destitution he so well knew.

During Mr. Bloomer's rectorship, we read that a glebe
was purchased by the parish. As this is a part of our
history we must record how this was done. It was resolved to raise funds by a lottery under the then existing
Colonial laws. It was to be the "Church Glebe Lottery,"
with "not two blanks to a prize." The net proceeds of
the venture were nearly $2,000, with which was pur-
chased a farm of seventy acres of arable land, about
a mile from Jamaica. Church lotteries were common
at that time. In 1774 a lottery of £4,000 was projected
to "purchase a piece of ground and erect a church thereon for a congregation of the Church of England, which
now assemble in Horse and Cart street (now Williams),
N. Y." A month after, another lottery was "projected,
to erect a church in Brooklyn, under the patronage of the
Rector and Vestry of Trinity Church." This was the beginning of St. Ann's Church.

In 1770, Mr. Bloomer writes: "I preach at the three
churches of Jamaica, Newtown and Flushing, alternately,
and generally to crowded assemblies, who behave during
Divine service with the utmost decency and decorum.
The churches are neat, well-finished buildings, but those

of Newtown and Flushing rather small for the congregations."

Mr. Bloomer began his work at a critical period of our country's history—just after the enforcement of the Stamp Act. The old vestry-book of this parish bears the hated stamp which shows that a tax of four pence had been levied by the British Crown on the purchaser of the book.

The impending storm of the Revolution burst upon the Colonies, and the Church had to bear the popular odium against England's rule. Congregations were broken up and churches were closed. Many of the clergy were in exile or prison, or were watched and harassed as suspects. But during the whole period, except on five Sundays, Mr. Bloomer sustained the regular services in the three parishes. They were united in their rector. His hold upon their respect and affection was too firm to be disturbed. The confidence inspired by a godly and unselfish life enabled him to minister in peace and with success in his extended cure, whether in heart men were rebels or Tories.

The occupation of the three towns by the British army, after the disastrous battle of Long Island, no doubt contributed much to the quietness of the three parishes. Flushing had its contingent of the army. A regiment of Hessians had winter quarters at Black Stump, and the place of their encampment was long known as the "hut lots." An excavation marked the spot where an ox was roasted when the Duke of Clarence (afterward William IV.) presented a stand of colors to the Hessian troops. Our own church-yard yielded its grim evidence of war when the excavation was made for the new church. In a supposed unused part of the yard a row of stalwart skeletons was exhumed. The fractured bones, the buttons and pieces of tobacco pipes indicated the unceremo-

nious burial of soldiers who had died of wounds. Some
descendants may tell, as a family tradition, how an an-
cestor fell in the old war and was buried in Flushing,
across the sea.

The war must have greatly reduced the material resources of the parish. David Colden said that when the
army of Gen. Clinton left Flushing in 1780, there "was

PRAYER BOOK, 1771.—THE PRAYER FOR THE PRESIDENT COVERING THE
PRAYER FOR THE KING.

not a fourfooted animal but dogs, nor a wooden fence
left in town." The final evacuation of Flushing, at the
close of the war, is thus described by a contemporary:
" In the morning there were thousands of soldiers around.
In the afternoon they were all gone, and it seemed lone-
some."

Among the treasures of the parish is a Prayer Book
"donated by Rebecca Morrell, Little Neck, 1771." It
bears marks of long use, and has certain evidence of having been on the desk and in use before and after it was
treason to pray for "Our most gracious Sovereign Lord,
King George." A paper on which is written the prayer
for "Thy servant, the President of the United States," is
pasted over the prayer for the king. This must have been
done after 1783, as Flushing was in possession of the
British troops during the Revolution, and those who read
the service had to give good heed as to which prayer they
used in those days.

Another relic of this period is the old vestry book above
referred to. This book was long lost. In 1895 it was
discovered by Captain F. A. Hinman among some old
books and papers in his house, and has been by him
kindly returned to the parish. The first record it con-
tains is dated 1770, and the last 1798. The book itself
is a small quarto of about seventy pages, and is bound in
paper covers of colored pattern, with the official stamp—
a crown surmounting an elaborate monogram, and
"paper, 4d." underneath.

In the first entry in this old book, appears the name of
Francis Lewis as church warden. He was one of the
signers of the Declaration of Independence. Mr. Lewis
was born in South Wales in 1712, and was educated at
Westminster. He early chose a mercantile life. The
American colonies were then the field for young and ad-
venturous spirits, and New York City the focus of activity
and energy. Young Lewis arrived there in 1737, and
established himself with the ample means at his com-
mand. He visited Europe, travelled extensively in Rus-
sia and other parts, and formed commercial relations in
various branches of trade. But the old French war came

on and a new field of adventure was opened. He took the contract to clothe the British army on the frontier and made headquarters at Oswego. His business knowledge made him a valuable aid in the transportation of ordnance and military supplies. But when Oswego was captured by Gen. Montcalm in 1757, Lewis was made a prisoner of war and was sent to France. It is not known when he returned, but in 1769 he appeared and led successfully in a matter of great importance to St. George's Church,* and was a church warden during the three following years. But the agitation which culminated in the Revolution had already begun. On his return he warmly espoused the cause of the patriots. He was not the man for half measures, and was early among the "sons of liberty," to inspire and lead on to action. In 1775 he was sent, from this State, to the Continental Congress, where he took a leading part; and, with his fellow patriots signed the memorable document that has made the names of the signers immortal.

A man of such influence and of such restless and daring activity, could not be otherwise than obnoxious to the government. He was marked as a dangerous rebel. The disastrous battle of Long Island had been fought, and New York City had fallen into the enemy's possession. The patriots were in hiding or exile. Mr. Lewis's family were on the farm in Flushing, and he was supposed to be with them. Mr. Lewis's farm consisted of about 200 acres, and was located where the village of Whitestone now stands. In the autumn of that year a company of British dragoons was sent to surprise and capture him. They surrounded his house, but he was conveniently

*Lewis headed the list of persons who pledged themselves to semi-annual payments for Mr. Bloomer's support. This paper was dated at Jamaica, May 23, 1769.

FIRST PAGE IN THE OLD VESTRY BOOK.

"not at home." They searched for criminating docu-
ments, and finding none, looted his house, burned his
papers and extensive library, and destroyed his furniture.
Worse than all, they took his accomplished wife captive
and held her as a hostage for her husband. A part of
the time she was without a bed or change of raiment.
Gen. Washington remonstrated against this, as inhuman
and contrary to honorable warfare, and Mrs. Lewis was
released ; but the shock and exposure caused her death.

Mr. Lewis was afterward employed by Congress to
purchase military stores for the army. He was sent by
Gen. Washington on various secret missions for which, by
his commercial knowledge and experience, he was well
fitted. After serving his country in this way to the end
of the war, he settled down to the quiet rural life of a
Flushing farmer. He had spent his fortune for his country during the war. He removed to New York in 1790,
and died there in poverty in 1803, aged ninety years,
having long outlived his earlier associates and friends.*

But to resume our direct history. A record of some
interest was made in 1782 : "At a meeting of the minis-
ter, church wardens and vestrymen of St. George's Church,
August 1, 1782, present, the Rev. J. Bloomer, rector, and
John Willet and David Colden, church wardens. and
Robert Crommeline, John Mackrell, Thos. Fairchild and
William Loweree, vestrymen, Mr. Crommeline informed
the vestry that the Hon. Samuel Cornel, Esq., of North
Carolina, late deceased, had by his last will piously given

---

*Other members of the vestry were prominent in public affairs at
this period. John Willet (warden) was arrested as a British sympa-
thizer, taken to Philadelphia, later imprisoned in New York, and
finally released for lack of evidence against him. Nathaniel Tom
(vestryman) was a member of the Provincial Congress in 1775. David
Colden (vestryman) was a son of Cadwallader Colden, President of
the Provincial Council. We find David Colden's name on Gen.
Greene's "List of Tories."

£200 for the use of this church, and that the Hon. Henry White, Esq., an executor, had informed him that he was ready to pay the legacy to any person authorized to receive it. Whereupon the vestry do appoint Mr. Robert Crommeline to receive the legacy, and the said Robert Crommeline is hereby authorized to place the £200 at interest in the hands of the corporation of Trinity Church, New York, and to take the bond of the said corporation for it, payable to the inhabitants of the Town of Flushing in communion of the Church of England as by law established." Concerning the final disposition of this money, the parish records give us no information.

This, we believe, was the first legacy received by St. George's Church.

The connection of Mr. Crommeline's name with this pious gift, brings another incident to mind. On the interior wall of the church, near the south porch, there is a tablet in memory of Mr. Robert Crommeline, who died in 1791. He was long an active and devoted member and benefactor of the parish. A copy of his will has a clause in it which reads thus : "I give and bequeath to the inhabitants of the Town of Flushing the sum of one thousand pounds as a fund for the support of the minister of the Protestant Episcopal Church, in the Town of Flushing for the time being, to be raised out of my real and personal estate." This will is dated, February 8, 1789. No record exists that this legacy was ever received.

After the United States had gained their independence, Mr. Bloomer was very active in those preliminaries which resulted in the organization of our American Church.

In October, 1784, there was a "voluntary meeting of sundry members of the Corporation for the Relief of Widows and Orphans."

After the business of this important charity was fin-

ished, the meeting resolved itself into an assembly of
"several members of the Episcopal Church, both of the
clergy and laity from the states of New York, New Jersey
and Pennsylvania." A committee of correspondence was
appointed "for the purpose of forming a continental representation of the Episcopal Church, and for the better

From Delafield's Life of Lewis.
FRANCIS LEWIS.

management of the concerns of said Church." Mr.
Bloomer was an active member of this primary assembly, and was appointed on this committee of correspondence. At a subsequent convention held in New York
we find, "from the united parishes of Jamaica, Newtown

and Flushing, on Long Island, the Rev. Mr. Bloomer and
Mr. Joseph Burrows, Mr. Charles Crommeline, Mr. Daniel Kissam and Mr. John Johnson." At this gathering it
was determined to appoint a committee of three clergymen " to wait upon the clergy of Connecticut, when con-
vened on the coming Trinity season, for the purpose of
soliciting their concurrence in such measures as may be
conducive to the union and prosperity of the Church."
The Church in Connecticut had stood aloof from the
Church in other states, and had acted for herself. In
1783, fourteen of her clergy had met at Woodbury and
secretly elected Dr. Seabury as their candidate for the
Episcopate. The secret was so well kept that, before it
became known, Dr. Seabury was on his way to England,
carrying a petition to the English bishops for consecration. Mr. Bloomer was appointed on this important committee, with the Rev. Benjamin Moore and the Rev.
Abraham Beach. The mission was successful and the
clergy of Connecticut sent a delegation of clergymen to
the General Convention which was to meet that year.
Connecticut did not approve of lay representation—and
to this day, departing from the general rule, has no lay-
men in the Standing Committee of the diocese. Besides
this very important mission, Mr. Bloomer was chosen
clerical delegate to every General Convention until his
death. Mr. Bloorme died in 1790. Before his death he
received from his Alma Mater the degree of S. T. D. He
was rector of the united parishes for more than twenty
years.

Among the articles deposited in the corner stone of
Grace Church, Jamaica, in 1861, is a plate from a de-
cayed coffin in the church-yard, inscribed, "Rev. Dr. J.
B." This was, without doubt, the coffin plate of the
Rev. Dr. Joshua Bloomer.

CHAPTER IX.

THE Rev. William Hammell, of Hackensack, N. J.,
succeeded Mr. Bloomer as Rector of the three parishes. He entered upon his duties August 1, 1790. with
a salary of $90. He was the first Rector of the three
parishes who had been ordained by an American bishop.
He was in deacon's orders when he came to Jamaica, and
was advanced to the priesthood in the following October.
Mr. Hammell's health was feeble and his eyesight im-
paired when he assumed the laborious charge of the three
parishes. In the first year of his pastorate he sought the
aid and comfort of a wife, marrying the widow of an offi-
cer of the English navy. To aid him further the vestries
bought him a "horse, saddle and bridle for $25." The
number of communicants in the parishes had been greatly
reduced by the war and other causes. At Jamaica, there
were twenty-one ; at Newtown, twenty-seven ; at Flushing, thirteen.

The vestries were called together at Jamaica in May,
1794. After service and a sermon the rector stated that
his salary was too small, and that he needed an assistant.
He had been called at a salary of £90 per year, "and as
much more as could be raised." The "as much more"

proved to be a myth. The vestries agreed, after confer-
ence, to raise his salary from £90 to £140. In the matter of an assistant, it was resolved that the vestries should
consult their respective congregations, and report at a
meeting to be held on Monday in Whitsun-week, at Jamaica. The members of the Flushing vestry present at
this meeting were : William Ustic (the grandfather of the
late Bishop Onderdonk), and Francis Lewis, church wardens ; Gerardus Beekman, John B. Hicks, John Hutchins
Smith and Thomas Fairchild, vestrymen. The proposed
meeting was prevented by a storm and the reports were
not heard.

In August, 1795, Mr. Hammell again called the vestries of the churches together for consultation. Great
dissatisfaction had arisen from the very imperfect manner in which the rector rendered the service. This was
because of defective sight and physical disability. He
laid before them his pitiable case. Partially paralyzed,
half blind and with little ability to perform the arduous
duties of his holy office, he asked for their counsel and
sympathy. What could be done ? Would they grant him
an assistant, or advise his resignation ? It was an affect-
ing scene. There were generous, humane and noble-
hearted men in those vestries. They considered his case
with tenderness and affectionate respect. The parishes
were poor, or at least they thought so. It had been difficult to give one minister a decent living. They could
only recommend his resignation. He bowed to their decision and resigned. But the vestries did not leave him
there. They voted to pay his salary to November. Then
they appealed to Trinity Church, New York, for help.
The appeal was signed by C. Smith, David Titus and
William Ustic, each a warden in one of the parishes con-
cerned.

The appeal met with a generous response.   It was resolved by the corporation of Trinity Parish : "That the
vestry grant to the Rev. Mr. Hammell, a paralytic at an
early period of his ministry and incapable of self-support,
£100 a year for thirty years."   This was a noble gift, and
its record on the minutes of that corporation stands as a

From Perry's History.
THE RT. REV. SAMUEL PROVOOST, D. D.

lasting testimony to its generosity and humanity.   The
period mentioned was a long one for "a paralytic in the
early period of his ministry," but Mr. Hammell lived
forty-five years after his resignation.   The following is
the obituary notice of the last rector over the three united

parishes : "Died : On the afternoon of Feb. 17, 1840,
after a short illness, the Rev. William Hammell of the
Episcopal Church, in the 78th year of his age"

In the October following Mr. Hammell's resignation
(1795), the vestries of the three parishes met at Jamaica,
and agreed to call the Rev. Thomas Lambert Moore, of
Hempstead. Their action in this was harmonious. But
there was an old controversy about the sale of a glebe.
The vestry of Jamaica had sold it years before, and Newtown and Flushing had claimed a portion of the money.
At this meeting it was proposed that Jamaica should apply the amount toward the purchase of another glebe, and
Newtown and Flushing would do their part in meeting
any deficiency. The Jamaica vestry would not agree to
this. All seemed to forget "How good and how pleasant it is for brethren to dwell together in unity !" The
old record states that "upon their refusal the church wardens and vestrymen of Newtown and Flushing went off
in a very abrupt and tumultuous manner, leaving the Jamaica vestry to themselves. The Rev. Mr. Moore declined the call, and recommended that the Rev. Charles
Seabury, a son of Bishop Seabury, be called for six months
on trial. The vestry of Jamaica acted on this suggestion
and Mr. Seabury accepted the call. He did not remain
longer than the time specified. He received $25 for his
services and $25 for his board. Flushing and Newtown
did not join in the call.

The parish of Newtown now formally withdrew from
the union of the three parishes, and carried out a long-
cherished plan of having a rector of its own. We do not
know how Jamaica and Flushing were again brought together. Jamaica appealed to the old friend of lame parishes, Trinity Church, New York, and obtained a response. An appeal was made at the same time by the

parish in Flushing with like success. Early in 1797, it was voted by Trinity Church : "That the treasurer pay the donation of £500 to the church in Flushing, the corporation of said church obligating itself to call a minister within fifteen months after the receipt of the donation ; and likewise within three years to vest the said sum of £500 in the purchase of a glebe." The same amount was given to Jamaica on similar conditions.

By the terms of the donation, each parish was separately to call a rector and separately vest money in a glebe within a specified time. Hence they did not unite in a call, but each parish gave a separate call to the Rev. Dr. Elijah D. Rattoone, Professor of Ancient Languages in Columbia College and Rector of St. Ann's Church, Brooklyn.   The call from Flushing read : "We, the church wardens and vestrymen of St. George's Church, Flushing, do hereby call the Rev. Elijah D. Rattoone as Rector of said Church, and on condition that Divine service be performed on every other Sunday during the three winter months, and once on each Sunday afternoon during the remainder of the year. We also covenant and agree to grant to the said clergyman the interest and use of £900 (providing that Trinity Church shall thereunto consent, as far as their approbation may be necessary), and on condition that satisfactory landed security shall be given for the same." The call from Jamaica was substantially the same, and granted him the use and interest of £900, "upon the principal being properly secured." Thus, by the terms of the calls, Dr. Rattoone would have £1,800 for his use, without interest. This he invested in a large farm and a spacious dwelling, on the road between Flushing and Jamaica. The conditions of the donation of Trinity were thus complied with, and that corporation, without doubt, approved of the action of the parishes.

The glebe thus provided—afterward known as "the Ezra Miller farm"—was really the personal property of Mr. Rattoone, subject to the lien of the bonds given to the parishes. At his resignation he offered it for sale, with this description: "For Sale: A country seat in Flushing, on the road from Jamaica, consisting of one hundred and ten acres. On it is a new house, forty-four by thirty feet, with a kitchen and servants' bed-rooms.

REV. ELIJAH D. RATTOONE'S RECTORY. A. D. 1797-1802.

It is on a lofty eminence with a view of Newtown, Flushing and its bay, the sound and Westchester, and the shore of New Jersey. The ground slopes from the house which overlooks the farm, and is approached by avenues of butternut and poplar trees. It has pear and cherry trees, and 1,200 peach trees planted from Prince's nursery. Inquire of Mr. Rattoone on the premises."

Mr. Rattoone was an accomplished scholar and eloquent preacher, of commanding presence and attractive manners. He ranked at the time among the most prominent of the clergy. He was long the secretary of the Convention of the Diocese of New York, and a member of its Standing Committee. Under his administration, the parish gathered strength and self-reliance. New life was infused and a more vigorous policy adopted. A new folio Prayer Book was ordered in the place of the old English Prayer Book, with its amended prayers and stained pages, which had been in use up to that time. The old book, and the (then) new one, are yet in the possession of the parish. The latter book is now a venerable and well-thumbed volume, bearing evidence of long and faithful use. It is of the first edition of the folio Prayer Book "published by direction of the General Convention." It was "printed by Hugh Gaine, at the Bible, Hanover Square, N. Y., 1795."

It may be of interest to know that Mr. Rattoone was appointed by the General Convention, with Dr. Moore of Newtown (afterward Bishop of New York), and the Rev. Mr. Beach, to revise and correct the sheets of the first Standard Book when going through the press.

At a meeting of the vestry, held August 15, 1797, the following resolutions were passed: "Resolved, that Oliver Bowne be allowed the sum of £6 per annum, and be supplied with sand and brooms, and be allowed the privilege of cutting the grass in the church-yard, on condition that he permits no cattle to run in the said yard, and keeps it clean, rings the bell at all Church times, or when called on, and keeps the church clean, windows, etc." "Resolved, that the clerk be allowed the sum of £6 per annum, and that Mr. Rattoone be requested to admonish him respecting his past irregular conduct, so as to prevent his transgressing after the same manner in future." This reference to the clerk reminds us of the arrangement of the chancel in those days. A long and high reading desk held the great Bible and Prayer Book. Behind and above the reading desk was the pulpit; below it was the clerk's stall. All this cumbersome furniture stood at the end of the chancel in the place now usually occupied by the altar. The altar, which was in the form of a table, stood before and below the clerk's stall. It was the clerk's duty to announce the psalm in metre, which was to be sung. This he did with the formula: "Let us sing to the praise and glory of God," such a psalm. He also led in the responses and frequently was the only person who responded at all. The congregation remained seated and it required the action of the House of Bishops, in 1814, to free those, who desired to stand during the act of praise, from the imputation of introducing "a dangerous ritual innovation." The usual vestments worn by the clergy were the cassock and black gown, with bands. There is evidence, however, that the surplice was worn in Flushing, from the time of Mr. Muhlenberg's rectorship.

In April, 1802, Mr. Rattoone laid before the vestry a call to St. Paul's Church, Baltimore, declared his intention to accept it, and asked them to provide a successor. By this act Jamaica and Flushing became vacant.

On June 22, 1802, the rite of Confirmation was for the first time administered in Flushing. The bishop was the Rt. Rev. Samuel Provoost, D. D. Ninety-seven persons were confirmed. The church was more than crowded. Representatives of three generations were among the candidates. Master and servant knelt for the same blessing. "Amelia, a slave, and Phebe, a freed woman," we find among the persons at this time confirmed.

After the resignation of Mr. Rattoone, the vestry of St. George's Church, resolved not to unite with the vestry of Jamaica in a call, "unless the vestry of that church discontinue the practice of obtaining subscriptions from the inhabitants of Flushing." Although the vestry of Jamaica promised to discontinue the objectionable practice, Flushing, for some unknown reason, preferred to unite with Newtown in the call of the Rev. Abram L. Clarke, of Rhode Island. This was done in April of 1803. In 1808

PITCH-PIPE, USED IN THE FIRST CHURCH.

we read that, according to an agreement between the two parishes, Mr. Clarke was to officiate at Newtown every Sunday morning and at Flushing every Sunday afternoon —from Easter to November. During the winter—from November to Easter—he was to give the third Sunday morning of each month to Flushing. Flushing was to contribute $300 toward his salary, and Newtown $450. But the arrangement was a brief one. In his address to the Convention of New York in 1809, Bishop Moore reported that, "the Rev. Abram L. Clarke, formerly rector of St. James's, Newtown, and St. George's, Flushing, is now confined to Newtown.   Flushing has, of course, become vacant."   Thus all official union between the parishes ceased.   It had existed for a century.   And thus ended a constant source of irritation and strife.   Mr. Clarke died on the last day of December, 1810, after a lingering illness, aged forty-two years.

CHAPTER X.

THE ACADEMY.

OUR history would be incomplete without a notice of
the old Academy, whose beginning was in these
days (1803). Many may not know that St. George's
Church had an academy of its own for many years. Early
in the history of the parish, Mr. John Aspinwall established a "Latin School" in connection with the church,
and engaged a competent teacher, who was also a lay-
reader. We have already spoken of him in chapter sixth.

The Academy stood on the church grounds, on the corner of what is now Main and Locust streets. The old
church stood much nearer Lincoln street than the present edifice. The Academy was a plain and unpretentious
building of two stories, in architecture more suggestive of
a factory than a school. In 1803, the sum of $520 had
been subscribed toward its erection. As this was about
the time of Dr. Rattoone's resignation, he evidently began the work. Interest had been enlisted and a plan
formulated during his incumbency. The building was
erected, and so far all things were ready. His successor,
Mr. Clarke, resided in Newtown, had many duties and
feeble health, and could give only a limited and interrupted oversight. He lacked the energy and experience
of his more scholarly predecessor. The parish itself had
exhausted its resources in building, and could do little
toward the support of proper teachers. In 1805 the build-

ing, with the land on which it stood, and the uncollected
pledges, was conveyed by the vestry, for the term of nine
hundred and ninety-nine years, to John H. Smith, Daniel
Bloodgood, Thomas Philips, William Prince, David Gard-
ener and Samuel H. Van Wyck, "at the annual rent of
six cents when legally demanded." In effect these gentlemen became a board of trustees, and the parish was

released from all care and responsibility. They called
the Academy, "Hamilton Hall." The record of a sur-
render to the vestry of some stock for the right of a small
family plot in the church-yard, leads us to infer that
shares had been sold to aid the school. The school was
in operation for many years, and the young persons of
the parish and village received the elements of what was

then called a good education. In those days the Academy was, no doubt, comparatively a pretentious building, and its course of study superior to the ordinary public school. The teachers in "Hamilton Hall" seem to have been men of intelligence and worth, and were generally successful as instructors. The teachers, the books and the birch were well remembered by many who were living when the writer came to Flushing.

In 1806 the parish loaned the proprietors $1,000, taking, for security, their joint bond and a mortgage on the land. But, notwithstanding this loan, and the lease of 999 years at a ground rent of six cents a year, the school was not a financial success. In 1810 the vestry purchased the lease and good will of the concern for $1,125, on condition that the proprietors would subscribe $125 toward repairing and refurnishing the building. Thus the Academy came back to the parish for the sum that had been loaned the proprietors. The vestry determined to establish an efficient and self-sustaining school, and hoped to derive some benefit to the parish treasury. Every effort was made to procure good teachers. But in spite of every effort the net proceeds dwindled. Other schools of private enterprise sprang up and, after a few years' struggle, it was discovered that a parish vestry could not always successfully carry on an unendowed school. The Academy was eventually closed, and the important purpose for which it had been erected was abandoned.

At that time a room for the Sunday School was much needed, and the Academy was altered to fit it for this purpose. The partitions in the upper story were removed, and a large Sunday School filled it, while an infant class occupied the lower story. The lower room was also used for evening lectures and services, during the week. This part of the building was called the chapel. Unpretentious as it was, it was generally well filled. The writer holds in pleasant and grateful memory the devout and attentive congregations that assembled there, and the interest manifested in the adult Bible class.

When the present church was built and the former restored as a chapel, the Academy building was sold and removed. The old landmark, so familiar to three generations, became a thing of the past. Old associations, not its architectural beauty, made some feel its loss. It found its way to what was then known as "Crow Hill," where it is still doing good service as a comfortable tenement house, on the southwest corner of Washington and Garden streets.

CHAPTER XI.

THE withdrawal of Mr. Clarke, in 1809, left Flushing dependent upon its own resources. Although independent in its corporate capacity, it had always united with one or both of the two neighboring parishes for ministerial service. A crisis had come. The interruption in the services, during the past few years, occasioned by the physical disability of the rector, had dispirited the congregation and greatly decreased the attendance. The outlook was depressing. But the few resolved to strike out manfully, stem the current and call a rector. They met in November, 1809, and their first act was a righteous one. Mr. Daniel Bloodgood was "appointed to settle all accounts with the late rector." They then proceeded to elect his successor. It was voted : "That the Rev. Barzillai Buckley should be called as rector of St. George's Church for the term of one year, and $550 be allowed as his salary for that term."

The call was accepted and the rector soon began his duties in the parish. The choice proved to be a very happy one. The people received their new rector with cordiality and confidence. He was their own, in undivided pastoral care, and he soon won their respect and love. His ministry began a new era in the history of the

parish ; and his worth as a parish priest was soon discovered and appreciated.   Long before his term of one
year had expired, the vestry renewed his call as rector for
an unlimited term.   Another subject in his behalf came
up, i. e., the need of a parsonage.   We have already noted
that Trinity Church had given £500 ($1,250), on condi-
tion that, within a certain number of years, it should be

REV. BARZILLAI BUCKLEY'S RECTORY.   1800–1820.

invested in a glebe.   The vestry judiciously thought that a
comfortable parsonage within the village would comply
with the spirit of the condition.   They accordingly bought
a house and lot from Mr. Daniel Bloodgood, for $1,500.
The house was on Main street, near the church.   This
not only proved a comfortable home for the rector, but

materially aided his salary. This rectory was sold to
Miss Margaret Hyer in 1826. for $1,350. The building
is still standing, and has been converted into two shops
—Nos. 37 and 39 Main street.

During Mr. Buckley's rectorship the congregation worshipped in the old, or first, church.   It had been repaired
and the interior renovated in a churchly manner, while
Mr. Rattoone was rector.   But, as every vestry well
knows, repairs and renovation are often required.   These
had been neglected during Mr. Clarke's administration.
When his successor came, the building and its appointments for worship were discreditable.   As the congregation now assembled twice on Sunday, instead of once in
three weeks during the winter, the condition of the church
became a matter of shame.   The current expenses were
then provided for by subscriptions, and the so-called
"penny collections" on Sundays.   As some of the congregation were too modest to have their names on the subscription list, the tradition is that, to meet such cases, all
the pews were assessed one dollar a year, when regularly
occupied by the same family.   But this would not add to
the improvement fund, and the case was urgent.   After
long deliberation and discussion, the vestry resolved to
adopt an heroic measure, and assessed every pewholder
one dollar, to meet the expense of repairs.   Not knowing
how this would be received, it was resolved : "That Mr.
William Prince be appointed to explain the reason which
made this necessary."   There is no record of how Mr.
Prince approached the people and "explained," and dared
to ask for a dollar additional that year, toward making
the church comfortable and decent.   It is said that two
families gave up their pews in consequence.   Others
hinted at a change at the next election of the vestry.   A
pew-tax was as obnoxious to them as the tax on tea had

been to their ancestors.   Others thought the church good
enough.   It was pride that prompted the measure.   This
was told the writer, many years ago, by a venerable
church warden who, as a youth, attended the church during Mr. Buckley's rectorship.   Some, however, responded
to the appeal, and the repairs were made.   As we shall soon
take leave of that venerable edifice, and give a brief history of the building of its successor, a parting word will
not be out of place.   A description of it has been already

FOOT STOVE, USED IN THE FIRST CHURCH.

given from tradition.   We can not well imagine the dis-
comforts which were patiently endured by our more hardy,
and perhaps less fastidious and exacting, forefathers.   The
facilities for heating the old church must have been very
primitive and scanty.   Stoves were rude and rare, and
the use of anthracite coal began at a far later date.   Yet
congregations met for Divine worship during the proverb-
ially "old-fashioned winters" of that period, and endured the cold and discomfort for the Word's sake and
for the good of their souls.   The women used "foot

stoves " (which may yet be found as relics in the attics of old houses), or heated bricks and stones, to warm the feet. Kind people living near the church (and notably a church warden) made extra fires on cold Sunday mornings to supply the foot stoves with living coals. As late as 1847, the sexton reaped a good revenue by attending to these stoves during the cold season.

During the rectorship of Mr. Buckley, 1809–1820, Bishop Hobart visited the parish, and administered the rite of Confirmation three times. His diocese then included the whole of the State of New York. His first visitation was in 1812, ten years after Bishop Provoost's first and only visit. Mr. Buckley presented forty-three candidates. Bishop Hobart's next official visit was in 1815, when fourteen were confirmed. The third visit was in 1819, at which time thirty were confirmed, making eighty-seven in seven years. After Mr. Buckley's death, nearly ten years passed without Confirmation, although the Bishop visited the parish triennially.

Mr. Buckley continued to labor among his people until his death, a period of more than eleven years. When the writer came to Flushing, some of his parishioners were living, and bore ample testimony to his faithfulness and loving kindness. Although he was a man of very respectable attainments and learning, he was not what would now be called a brilliant preacher. Yet his daily life and godly conversation preached a constant and eloquent sermon. His was a gentle and loving nature, marked by great humility and sincerity. He was a loyal churchman and strove to lead his people in the good "old paths." He died at the age of forty-one. Bishop Hobart, in his address to the Convention of New York, in 1820, said: "I have to record the death of the Rev. Barzillai Buckley, Rector of St. George's Church, Flush-

ing, who united in an eminent degree primitive Church
principles with primitive humility and piety. ' The Bishop
visited him during his last illness, and officiated at his
funeral in the church, on Good Friday afternoon, 1820.
He was buried beneath the chancel of the church. The
Rev. Evan M. Johnson, then the Rector of St. James's
Church, Newtown, preached the funeral sermon. A mural
tablet on the right side of the chancel, erected by his
widow, perpetuates his name. He came to the parish in
its depression and weakness. When called to his reward,
the parish had taken a permanent position among the
prosperous parishes of Queens County.

BAPTISMAL BOWL, USED AT AN EARLY DATE IN ST. GEORGE'S CHURCH.

Mr. Buckley's successor was the Rev. J. V. E. Thorne.
He took temporary charge of the parish in June, 1820.
At a vestry meeting, held August 7th of that year, two
members being absent, it was "resolved unanimously
that the Rev. J. V. E. Thorne be presented with a call
from this church, and that the secretary be requested to
address him a letter to that effect." The record goes on
to say : "The secretary pro tem. then wrote the following letter which, being read, was approved : 'To the Rev.
John V. E. Thorne. Dear Sir—At a meeting of the War-

dens and Vestry of St. George's Church, Flushing, L. I.,
held on the 27th of July, it was unanimously determined
to present you with a call from this church, and at a subsequent meeting of the congregation on Sunday, the 30th,
the same unanimous determination was expressed by
them. I am, in consequence, directed by the wardens
and vestry to acquaint you with the same, and to express
their sincere wishes that nothing may occur to prevent
your acceptance of it. Your salary (agreeably to a resolution of the vestry), in consequence of your former services, commenced on the 18th of June last. By order of
the Wardens and Vestry of St. George's Church, Flushing.

I am, your obedient servant,

THOMAS MARSTON,

8th August, 1820. Secretary pro tem.'"

The meeting then adjourned to 9 o'clock the next morning.

It would appear from this letter that the congregation
united with the vestry in calling Mr. Thorne. For such
a procedure, neither the charter of the parish, the laws of
the state, nor the canons of the Church make any provision. We must look upon the action, therefore, as simply
a desire on the part of the vestry to act in accordance
with the wish of the congregation. The authority and
responsibility could not, by the vestry, be shared with or
delegated to other persons.

CHAPTER XII.

THE vestry meeting, referred to in the last chapter, adjourned to the following morning. This adjourned meeting was held to consider the subject of building a new church. The extract from the minutes of the meeting, given below, is the first recorded intimation of such a purpose. There are no minutes recorded from March 25, 1818, to April 12, 1820. The record says: "At the adjourned meeting on Tuesday morning, August 8, 1820, the members present proceeded to examine the proposals which had been sent in for building a new church. Two only were handed them—one by Benjamin Lowerre and one by James Morrell. The vestry, after due consideration, resolved that the proposal of James Morrell be the one that shall be accepted. Resolved, that a committee of three persons from the vestry be chosen to enter into a contract with James Morrell to build the church agreeably to the plan advertised. Resolved, that Thomas Philips, James Bloodgood and Isaac Peck be the said committee. Resolved, that the church shall be erected on a site between the present one and the academy, and that the said committee have authority to fix upon the same. Resolved, that the committee be authorized to collect the moneys which have been, or may hereafter be, subscribed toward the building of the said church."

The records do not tell us when, or by whom, the subject of building a new church was first introduced to the
vestry. The subject had probably been long considered,
and the official record of the vestry gives us the results of
patient and energetic work on the part of men and women
of the parish. A vote of thanks to Mr. Thomas Bloodgood, and friends in New York, for generous subscriptions
and kind interest, tells us that aid was received outside
of Flushing. We have no data from which to learn the
cost of the new edifice. The site chosen by the committee was where the present stone church stands. Large
Locust trees stood between the old church and the academy, some of which were cut down to give place for the
new building. The materials for the second church were
of the best quality. The corner posts were of white oak,
and the main timbers of Georgia pine, sawed by hand on
the meadows near the bridge. They were taken from
a raft of logs which had been brought up from New York.
The old church remained in use until the completion of
its successor. It was condemned to be torn down after
more than eighty years of service. Mr. David T. Waters
related to the writer, that at the time, 1820, he was an
apprentice to the builder of the new church, and aided in
the work. He climbed up inside of the tall steeple of the
old church and fastened the rope by which it was to be
pulled down. Three feet of snow covered the ground at
the time. When the old land-mark came crashing down,
it was dashed into fragments. Mr. Waters recovered the
vane and ball, with the iron work, and they were carefully restored and placed on the new church. They may
be seen on the belfry of the chapel to-day. The "roos-
ter" is still faithful after a service of nearly one hundred
and fifty years.

Thus ends the story of the first church of St. George's

parish. The older members left it with some regret. It had long stood as the only house of worship, except the Friends' Meeting House, in the whole Town of Flushing. Tender memories clustered around it. Generations had worshipped there. Beneath its shadows rested their dead. Its bell had called the people to prayers, had rung out the merry marriage peal and had tolled the requiem of the departed.

The new building progressed rapidly. The late Mrs. Garretson said she well remembered when the men of the parish assembled to "raise" the framework, and afterward lunched on the grounds of her father, opposite the church. Mr. Thorne reported to the diocesan convention in October, 1820, that the new church would probably be ready for consecration during the coming May or June. Bishop Hobart, in his address to the convention, held in 1821, said: "The respectable congregation of St. George's Church, Flushing, L. I., one of the oldest in the state, having erected a new church edifice for worship, in a style of neatness and convenience that does them great credit, I consecrated it to the service of Almighty God according to the forms of our Church, on Friday, May 25th." (1821.)

The Christian Journal reported some particulars of the consecration: "Morning Prayer was conducted by the Rev. Thomas Brientnall, Rector of Zion Church, N. Y. The lessons were read by the Rev. H. U. Onderdonk, Rector of S. Ann's Church, Brooklyn, and an appropriate discourse was delivered by the bishop, who was attended in this interesting and impressive solemnity by a number of the clergy. St. George's Church is built near the site of an edifice of the same name, the decayed state of which rendered necessary the erection of the new edifice. For the accommodation of the increased and increasing num-

THE SECOND ST. GEORGE'S CHURCH, BUILT 1821, NOW USED BY THE
SUNDAY SCHOOL.

bers, the second edifice is of considerably larger dimensions than the former, and it is furnished in a much neater style. It is a neat and commodious building, very creditable to the taste and skill which planned and executed it."

It appears, then, that the new church was begun in August, 1820, and was completed and ready for consecration in May, 1821. In 1839, to meet the demands of an increasing congregation, an addition of seventeen and a half feet was made, at a cost of about $1,750. This sum was raised by subscription and by the sale of a few of the additional pews. Thus, under the energetic leadership of Mr. Thorne, a new church was built and a new era of Church life dawned on the parish.

Mr. Thorne came from a manly ancestry—a race undaunted by difficulties, and self-assertive when rights were invaded. His inherited virtues would not be dwarfed by disuse in older Flushing. He was chairman of the building committee for the new church in fact, as well as ex officio. He made quite an innovation in the arrangement of the chancel and its furniture. In the rural churches of the day, the reading desk was placed within the sanctuary, and the holy table, or altar, was in front of the desk. The pulpit had its place above desk and altar. Mr. Thorne placed the reading desk outside the chancel rail, and the holy table conspicuously within, where it belonged. This brought some censure, which he little regarded. On his retirement, the first act of the vestry was to change this arrangement, and to restore the desk to its old place in the sanctuary.

In addition to the care of the parish and the building of a new church, Mr. Thorne built a mansion for himself, which has long stood among the more prominent dwellings in older Flushing. It is now the residence of Mrs. Joseph

Fitch, near Main street, and between Amity and Locust streets. Mr. Thorne was evidently preparing for a long residence in Flushing.

But his rectorship was not a long one, and came to a close rather abruptly. We know something of the causes which led up to it. It seems that a spot near his residence was used as a dumping ground. Expostulations and vigorous protests were unheeded until the extreme limit of his forbearance was passed. Meeting the authors of the intolerable nuisance on the town dock, he threatened then and there to quicken their sense of right and justice by a little muscular reasoning. The hasty parson may have spoken unadvisedly with his lips. The challenged party chose the better part of valor, and made a charge to the vestry against the belligerent rector. A meeting was called, and it was resolved, that a communication, in writing, be sent to the Rev. Mr. Thorne, on "subjects" which have come to the knowledge of the vestry. This letter was signed by each member of the vestry. The time for the Easter election drew near. Mr. Thorne's answer awaited the result. After an excited election, the retiring board was returned by the congregation. The rector called a meeting and asked leave of absence for two or three months. It was granted. He then "stated his intention of resigning at no distant period." On his return to Flushing, he called a vestry meeting, and stated his intention of resigning on that day. A large arrearage of salary was due. It was, therefore, resolved : " That the vestry settle the account, and pay in full for his services." " Mr. Thorne then handed in his resignation dated this day (July 1, 1826.) It was moved that the resignation be accepted." " The Rev. Mr. Thorne having withdrawn, and all the wardens and vestrymen being present, it was resolved : ' That a call be presented to the Rev. Wm. A. Muhlenberg, of Pennsylvania, and that the clerk address him a letter to that effect.' Carried unanimously."

Mr. Thorne's ministry of six years was energetic and successful. He built a new church and aroused a sluggish congregation into activity. His ploughshare may have been sharp, but he turned up an overrun and fallow field, and prepared it for his eminent successor. Only one side of the man has been seen in our sketch. There was another side—a genial and gentler side. The writer found some of his parishioners still surviving, when he entered the same field. They held their early pastor in affectionate regard, and recalled his memory with grateful respect.

Arrearage in pew rents was a very prominent subject of discussion in the vestry during Mr. Thorne's rectorship. In 1825 a special committee on finance reported as due for pew rent, uncollected, $340. This was when the annual rental was $413.50. The pews ranged from $3 to $10 per year, with sixty-four persons leasing pews. There was also due on uncollected subscriptions for the new church, $563, most of which was subsequently paid. It was during that year, 1825, that a vote of thanks was given by the vestry " to Mrs. Effingham Lawrence and family, for the liberal donation of land adjoining the church-yard." Mrs. Lawrence was the mother of the late Hon. John W. Lawrence, long a church warden of St. George's Church.

CHAPTER XIII.

A S stated in the preceding chapter, the same meeting
that accepted Mr. Thorne's resignation elected his
successor— the Rev. William Augustus Muhlenberg. Mr.
Muhlenberg was born in Philadelphia in 1796, and was
baptized by Dr. Helmuth, a Lutheran divine. He was
the great-grandson of the Rev. Henry M. Muhlenberg, the
venerable founder and "Patriarch of the Lutheran Church"
in this country, who came from Germany in 1742. His
father's name was Peter M. Muhlenberg, who was also a
Lutheran minister. While Peter M. Muhlenberg was settled at Blue Ridge, Va., as pastor of the Lutheran congregation, he, under the influence of his friends, Gen. Washington and Patrick Henry, laid aside the ministry for the
army. The last sermon he preached was on the duties
men owe to their country. An immense congregation
filled the church and church-yard. His closing words
were: "There is a time for everything—a time to preach
and a time to fight—and now is the time to fight." Suit-
ing his action to his words, he threw off the clerical gown
and stood before his congregation in full uniform as a
warrior, and read his commission as a colonel in the Continental army.

The Rev. William A. Muhlenberg—the son of this fight-
ing Lutheran minister—took Orders in the Episcopal

Church, and was Rector of St. James's Church, Lancaster, Pa., for five years. He resigned his rectorship, that he might devote some time to the study of the schools of Europe. Leaving Lancaster, he came to New York for a brief visit before sailing for Europe. While in the study of his old friend, Dr. Milnor, a gentleman from Flushing

THE REV. WILLIAM A. MUHLENBERG, D. D.

came in. He was one of the vestry of St. George's Church, who had come to ask Dr. Milnor if he could recommend a clergyman for the vacant pulpit of St. George's, on the morrow. The Doctor, turning to Mr. Muhlenberg, said: "Could not you go?" He readily assented, little thinking that it would change all his plans and open a path to the realization of what had become the leading idea of his life. He came as a temporary supply, without the remotest idea of taking a rural parish, much less of spending eighteen years of active life in Flushing. The rector, Mr. Thorne, returned from his vacation soon after, and resigned. Mr. Muhlenberg was immediately elected to the rectorship. After some hesitation, he accepted and entered upon his duties in August, 1826.

It was during the first year of Mr. Muhlenberg's rectorship, that the method of electing vestrymen was changed from a *viva voce* vote to the secret ballot. When he came to Flushing he established himself at the only village hotel, known as the "Pavilion." He brought with him two favorite boys who had been monitors under him in Lancaster—one of them was James B. Kerfoot, afterward the Bishop of Pittsburg, the other was Libertus Van Bokkelen, who became a celebrated scholar and teacher. Both were long associated with him in educational work. Sitting one day with them in the public dining room, he overheard some gentlemen talking about building an academy in Flushing, as a family and boarding school for boys. It struck the favorite subject of his thoughts and life. He joined them and, without premeditation, offered himself to take the charge of such a school, if they would erect the building he desired. In the evening, to his surprise, they called at his rooms to say that they would accept his proposition. He promised to have plans drawn for the proposed building. It was to be erected and owned by an incorporated company, and to be called, "The Christian Institute of Flushing." But when the bill for its incorporation was brought to the Legislature, the gentlemen in charge feared that the title, "Christian," might prejudice some sensitive members against it, and asked permission to change the title to that of "The

Flushing Institute." Mr. Muhlenberg consented to the change.

The corner-stone of the Institute was laid August 11, 1827. Among other objects put into the box, was a Greek Testament, inscribed with these words : "Believing that the Gospel of Jesus Christ is the best knowledge, the true wisdom, and the only foundation of moral virtue, we deposit this New Testament in the original language, praying that its faith may ever be the corner-stone of education in this Institute." The prayer has been signally answered, for hardly a day has passed since it was built, that it has not been used as a Christian school, and the faith of the Gospel made the corner-stone of its education. It is so now, and so may it ever be !

Mr. Muhlenberg still retained his position as Rector of St. George's, though his duties at the Institute necessarily required much of his time. He signified his desire to resign as soon as a successor could be elected. At a meeting in December, 1828, the vestry made an attempt to choose a rector in his place. Their choice fell on the Rev. Mr. Dorr, of Lansingburg, but it was not unanimous. Understanding this, Mr. Dorr declined the call. Mr. Muhlenberg agreed to remain until his successor could be chosen, if the vestry would relieve him on Sunday afternoons. This was done, and the Rev. Mr. S. Seabury took his place at Evening Prayer. Early in 1829 the Rev. William H. Lewis was called as rector. This released him from all pastoral duty and left him free to devote himself to his educational work. There had been some beginnings of Sunday School work before Mr. Muhlenberg's day, but it was he who gave it definite form and life. The Sunday School first met in the building on Lincoln street, held in trust by the "Flushing Female Association."

The Institute was successful and soon paid expenses. Its reputation extended : pupils came from all parts of the land. But Mr. Muhlenberg soon evolved larger plans to carry out his ideal of higher, Christian education. He purchased a farm of 175 acres, at what is now College Point, where he designed to erect, at a cost of $50,000,

THE FLUSHING INSTITUTE, BUILT 1828.

a stone edifice for a college. The foundation was begun, and on October 15, 1836, the corner-stone was laid with jubilant services and enthusiastic anticipations. The goal of his life's ambition seemed in sight. But it was never reached. God had other purposes for him to fulfil. The building went no further than the foundation. The commercial upheaval of 1837 came on, and his financial supporters were involved in the ruin. A wooden structure was built not far from the foundation of the college for a grammar school, the ruins of which are still known as the "College." The pupils at the Institute were removed to this building, and all connection with Flushing ceased.

Dr. Muhlenberg was intimately connected with many reforms and improvements in the Church. The first Church Hymnal largely owed its existence to his agitation and counsel. He was also the author of several well known hymns. His influence and example did much toward the revival, in this country, of the Apostolic custom of weekly celebrations of the Holy Communion. He was the champion of the free-pew movement, and declined an urgent invitation of the vestry to preach the sermon at the consecration of the new church in his old parish of Flushing, because the auctioneer was to sell or lease its sittings to the highest bidder. Truly did the Bishop of Central New York say of him, at the time of his death : "With a force individual and single, and a self-forgetfulness that seemed absolute, he made a place for himself in the priesthood of this Church, and in the attachment of its members which was altogether characteristic, and it is left empty by his removal. Without being a theologian or statesman, he was greater than either, and while apparently wrong in some opinions, he comprehended as few men living or dead have, what the worship and work of this Church in America ought to be."

He died in 1877, and was buried at St. Johnland, where his remains lie in the midst of the graves of old pilgrims and crippled children—former inmates of the home he had established as his last great work. His monument bears his own chosen inscription : "I know Whom I have believed."

CHAPTER XIV.

THE REV. WILLIAM H. LEWIS. A. D. 1829–1833.

A T a vestry meeting, held February 5, 1829, the Rev. W. H. Lewis was elected rector for one year, and the clerk was directed " to give notice to Mr. Lewis of his election, and to request him to take charge immediately." The election was far from being unanimous. Two of the vestry present requested their protest to be recorded against the action ; and a third absented himself, foreseeing what would be the result of the meeting. Mr. Lewis came to a divided congregation. There was no objection to him personally. At that time the Church in the United States was divided into two well defined parties. One party was called " High Church," and the other " Low Church." Mr. Lewis was considered a Low Churchman, and, for that reason, his election was opposed by a part of the vestry. In both parties were men of unquestioned piety and loyalty.

At this time, there were but two religious organizations in Flushing—the Society of Friends and St. George's Church. Hence there was a large number of persons who claimed an interest in the Church, because they were not Quakers. Their influence was used to disturb, more frequently than to assist, the Church. They claimed the ministrations of the rector, when needed ; and attempted to influence his action by their activity at the Easter election. They were not Churchmen by conviction, nor were they frequently seen at public worship.

Mr. Lewis began his ministry with energy and zeal.
He was known to be a Low Churchman, and was elected
as such. His faithful appeals aroused, if they did not
convict. He was young, he had zeal, and he soon adapted
himself to his new field. The term of his call, as rector
for one year, began to draw toward its close. Meanwhile,
a vestry election had increased the majority friendly to
him. At a vestry meeting in December, 1829, a tentative
motion was made : "That at the next meeting of the
vestry, they should take into consideration the permanent
call of the Rev. Mr. Lewis, as rector of this church."
After a warm debate, it was resolved : "That the vestry
will attend to this motion at its next meeting." That next
meeting was held on March 6, 1830, two days before the
expiration of the rector's year—a delay of three months.
At that meeting, "agreeably to a motion made at the last
meeting for 'giving a permanent call to the Rev. W. H.
Lewis as rector of this church,' the same was taken into
consideration, and the vestry being informed that a part
of the congregation was opposed to a permanent call, a
motion was made and carried that Mr. Lewis be called as
rector of this church for the term of eight years, from the
eighth day of this month." The laurels of this victory
were about equally divided. Mr. Lewis entered his new
term of office with renewed energy. His native characteristic of patience and quiet firmness was proof against
all opposition. He had long seen that the vice of intemperance was the bane of Flushing. He invited Dr. Mc-
Ilvaine, then Rector of St. Ann's, Brooklyn, and afterward
Bishop of Ohio, to come to Flushing and deliver a lecture
in St. George's Church, on the evils of intemperance. On
a week-day evening, the eloquent preacher appeared. A
great congregation filled the church. Among those present
were many whose faces were more frequently seen in the

bar-room than in God's sanctuary.   They were not pleased
with the lecture.   In the common room of the village inn
the subject was discussed, and it was decided to record
this disapprobation at the next Easter election.   This
they did, and all the members of the vestry supposed to
be friendly to the rector, were defeated.   Among the newly

THE REV. WILLIAM H. LEWIS, D. D.

elected was " mine host" of the village hostelry, and
another was the quiet counsellor in the conclave, who had
proposed the *coup-de-main*, and who was chosen as clerk
and treasurer of the vestry.   The interests of the parish
were handed over to new men, and the congregation was
left to reap the good or the evils resulting from their over-

indulgence, or inattention to the affairs of their church. The relations between Mr. Lewis and his new vestry were peaceable, if not always harmonious. Acts of petty opposition occurred, but the young rector exercised the charity that "beareth all things." The work he had to do was too great for him to come down and chase to its death every phantom of idle gossip.

The parish embraced a wide territory. The outlying neighborhoods of the village, with the exception of some scattered Church families, were a sort of "*in partibus infidelium*," unvisited and neglected. Mr. Lewis felt that his ministry must include these also. He began a house to house visitation, much to the surprise of some, in whose humble homes a minister of the Gospel had never before been seen. Among the localities visited, one was then called "Cookie Hill." The name is now obsolete, having been changed, first, to Clintonville, and then, embracing a wider territory, to Whitestone. Mr. Lewis visited the homes and proposed a weekly, or occasional, visitation, when in some house he could meet the assembled neighbors. Quite a number became interested in these meetings. The dormant conscience was awakened, and these outside services became the hopeful beginning of a better state of things. Households were baptized. Among the Church families that the writer found as worshipers in St. George's Church, not a few were the fruits of the work in these prayer meeting ministrations. From the seed thus sown in this neglected locality, a harvest was ultimately reaped in the establishment of the parish of Grace Church, Whitestone.

Two years passed, and at Easter, 1833, a change in the vestry was made. By an almost unanimous vote, the friends of Mr. Lewis were elected. During the preceding year the cholera, in its first visitation (1832), had

appeared in Flushing.   Mr. Lewis had taken the lead in
ministering to the stricken. Men's thoughts were directed
to other and higher things than party strifes in the Church.
Meanwhile a steady and visible change was taking place
in the religious life of the congregation.   Some acces-
sions from abroad had introduced a more active and ag-
gressive religious zeal.   New communicants were added,
the disaffected were won back, and a state of peace was
promised.

In July, 1833, Mr. Lewis received a call to St. Michael's Church, Marblehead, Mass., and tendered his resignation as Rector of St. George's parish.   The vestry was
unwilling to accept his resignation, and offered to make
his rectorship unlimited ; but at his earnest request it
yielded and released him.   This was done at a meeting
held August 3, 1833.   Thus ended a troubled, but successful and fruitful rectorship of nearly five years.

CHAPTER XV.

ON September 3, 1833, the Rev. J. Murray Forbes
was elected to succeed Mr. Lewis. He accepted
the call, and entered upon his duties the first of October.
Although, on some subjects, he was supposed to hold
opinions which differed from his predecessor's, still he
guided his course with a wisdom and moderation which
disappointed both parties. He would be of no party.
He came to build up and to heal, not to divide. He carried on the work very much as his predecessor had left
it. To a quiet personal dignity and social refinement he
added courtesy and cordiality of manner, and soon gained
the confidence and affectionate respect of his congregation. Party spirit was allayed, and a united people were
made ready to become co-workers with their rector. But
his rectorship was a brief one : before the end of a year
he accepted a call to St. Luke's Church, New York. Mr.
Forbes afterward became unsettled, by the controversies
of the time. On the death of his wife he decided to seek
admission to the ministry of the Church of Rome. When
St. Michael's (R. C.) Church, of this village, was dedi-
cated, in 1856, Father Forbes was the preacher. Not
many years after his departure from our branch of the
Church, Dr. Forbes began to discover that distance had
"lent enchantment to the view." Much had proved to

be disappointing and illusive. He was led to reconsider
the judgment upon which he had based his action ; and,
in the autumn of 1859, he withdrew from obedience to
the Papal See. On recantation and the renunciation of
allegiance to Rome, Dr. Forbes was restored to the exercise of the ministry he had forsaken. He was appointed
Dean of the General Theological Seminary, a newly established and responsible office, where he spent many
years with zeal and fidelity.

A rule of the vestry, made during Mr. Forbes's rectorship, explains itself. It was "that no nails be driven in
the walls of the church, or anything be posted thereon
only by the direction of the vestry." This was before the
era of carpets in the aisles of St. George's. The bare
floors often betrayed the state of the roads by the foot-
marks, for Flushing streets were unpaved at that time.
The pews were uncushioned, save at the provision of the
occupants. Those thus furnished often presented many
colors, and were generally well worn, as the cushions for
pews were an hereditary family possession. Mr. Forbes
had a high and almost fastidious sense of neatness and
propriety. Aisles stained with mud, and often with of-
fensive evidences of the use of tobacco, were intolerable.
To abate the nuisance and to lessen the sound of heavy
Sunday boots, he had the aisles thickly sprinkled with
white beach sand, which was renewed as needed. Sand
was widely used by neat housewives of that day on un-
carpeted floors, and gave a neat appearance to unsightly
boards.

Soon after Mr. Forbes's departure—September 1, 1834—
the vestry elected the Rev. Samuel R. Johnson, of Hyde
Park, at a salary of $800 per annum. Mr. Johnson ac-
cepted and soon entered upon his duties. The vestry had
chosen a rare man. He began his work with loving zeal.

Very soon his congregation knew him—and to know
him was to love him.   His presence assured good will,
and his voice seemed to speak of peace.   Never before
had a rector entered the parish where the rough places so
soon became smooth, and the crooked places straight.
He won the love and confidence of all.   A new era of
peace and progress seemed to dawn upon St. George's.
But Mr. Johnson's rectorship, like that of his predecessor,
was short.   The following letter addressed to the vestry,
in October, 1835, explains itself:

OCTOBER 19, 1835.

"TO THE WARDENS AND VESTRYMEN OF ST. GEORGE'S,
FLUSHING.

DEAR BRETHREN :

It is not without painful feelings that I now formally
send to you my resignation of the rectorship of St.
George's Church, and ask you to accept it.   I should, indeed, be ungrateful, did I not part with regret from a
people among whom I have met with such uniform kindness and so hospitable reception ; where my imperfect
services have been so cordially welcomed ; and where
nothing has happened in any degree to interrupt our mutual good will and affection.   Nor could I find it in my
heart to part from you under present circumstances, except from this cause, that I feel myself after many anxious thoughts and much prayerful consideration, sum-
moned, by a conviction of duty which I dare no longer to
struggle against, to a more difficult field of labor.

And I feel the more, because I know the frequent
change of pastors leaves the parish in an anxious state,
and exposes it to the danger of a vacancy and of divided counsels ; and that the pastor cannot be so useful
for some time, when he and his people are but little ac-

quainted ; on which account I cannot but fear that my
very short residence has been of no advantage to the
parish, but has rather kept it back.　Permit me then, as
some reparation of the injury, and as sign of my good
will and affection, respectfully to return the recompense
I have received for my few and imperfect labors, and

THE REV. SAMUEL R. JOHNSON, D. D.

present unto your acceptance the accompanying papers,
which are just equal in pecuniary value to the salary of
the year.

And may the Lord Jesus be with you, Brethren ; guide
you with His counsel ; give you a pastor after His own

heart ; take you under His own keeping ; and bless you with the richest blessings of His grace, peace and salvation.

I remain with all affection and true regard, Yours, most faithfully,   SAMUEL R. JOHNSON."

The "accompanying papers, equal in pecuniary value to the salary of a year," were the assignment of a bond and mortgage to the vestry, to the amount of $800. Not the greatest "quid pro quo" member of the vestry could advocate its acceptance. It was resolved : "That we cannot consistently with our feelings, accept the assignment of the bond and mortgage offered to us by the Rev. S. R. Johnson, in consideration, as he is pleased to say, of his imperfect services during his ministry with us." The papers were returned, but that did not end the matter. In a record of the vestry, unfortunately without date, but soon after, "Mr. Isaac Peck communicated to the vestry that the Rev. Mr. Johnson had made a donation of $300 toward the erection of a building for the Sunday School, or for other purposes." The "other purposes" seem to have absorbed it, but the need of the building was in the retiring rector's mind. Early in his brief rectorship, by his inspiration, evidently, a resolution had been passed : "That when sufficient funds are subscribed, the vestry proceed to erect a suitable building for a Sunday School and such other purposes as they may deem proper." A committee was appointed, with power "to associate with them such other persons as may be desired." Something like a Parish House seemed to be in mind.

The resignation of Mr. Johnson was accepted by the vestry, with much reluctance. Such had been the relations between the rector and congregation from the beginning, that nothing but a conviction of duty on his

part, and stern necessity on theirs, could have dissolved
them.   At his own expense, Mr. Johnson went with the
Apostolic Kemper, to aid in laying the foundations of the
Church in what was then known as the "Far West."
Gladly would we follow him, did it not lead us from our
purpose.   Suffice it to say, that bishoprics were almost
forced upon him, which his humility and self-negation
compelled him to decline.   When, from the infirmities of
age, he was compelled to retire from the active duties of
a high position to which the Church had called him, it
was to finish his course in a humble rural parish.   There,
in his declining years, he endeared himself as he had
done in Flushing long before.

CHAPTER XVI.

THE REV. ROBERT B. VAN KLEECK—THE REV. FREDERIC J. GOODWIN—THE REV. GEORGE BURCKER. A. D. 1835-1847.

THE vestry meeting which accepted Mr. Johnson's resignation (October 20, 1835), resolved unanimously to elect the Rev. Robert B. Van Kleeck, of Fishkill Landing, as rector, at a salary of $800 a year. On the first of November, Mr. Van Kleeck answered the call: "I am now able to signify my acceptance of your gratifying invitation, with the hope and prayer that the unanimity which has marked your counsel in coming to a decision may be enjoyed in all our deliberations."

The new, and then young rector availed himself of the aid around him; and the Sunday School and increasing congregation soon manifested the wisdom of the vestry in their unanimous choice. The accommodations for the Sunday School were inadequate. Its growth was hindered. The church building (the present audience room of the chapel) was too small for the congregation. The rector "lived in his own hired house," and most of the parish appointments for Church services and work belonged to an older generation. It was time to move forward. The first step onward was to provide a suitable Sunday School building. At a vestry meeting, June, 1836, it was resolved: "That a committee of three be appointed to receive proposals for building a Sunday

School and lecture room for the church, and also to ascertain the expense of the removal and repair of the present building, and report." " The present building " was the old Academy, referred to in chapter tenth. It was two stories in height, very plain and factory-like in architecture, and far from being an ornament to the church

THE REV. ROBERT B. VAN KLEECK, D. D.

grounds. Some desired a new building, while the more conservative advocated the repair of the old Academy. It was resolved at a later vestry meeting : "That the Academy be removed and repaired." The committee on repairs was ordered to carry out the work. These changes have already been referred to in the tenth chapter. The cost of the whole was $1,180. No doubt, the people were well satisfied with their work

But another, and a pressing need existed. Flushing had few unoccupied houses; the parish had no rectory and was too large to be without one. The rectory on Main street had been sold in 1826. In August, 1836, a committee was appointed "to ascertain what a house twenty-six by thirty-four feet could be built for, and report at the next vestry meeting." The committee reported, "that Thomas Fowler's bid for $2,470, was the lowest." With this modest sum to raise, it was resolved to begin as soon as money could be collected. Meanwhile, the rector's salary was increased to $1,000, from the first of November, and the vestry "agreed to hire a house for him from this date for a year."

During 1837, an improvement was attempted in the grounds in front of the church. The only notice in the vestry book reads : " Resolved, that Isaac Peck and Robert Carter attend to having the wall put in front of the church." In olden time the street was little more than a country road. The church of 1821 stood a few feet above the street. In 1837, a broken fence and rude bank of turf were a delight for small boys and the village goats. This was the "front of the church," where the wall was to be built. It was built up to a level with the churchyard, and was of substantial structure. Two cargoes of stone were used, in addition to the local stone for the foundation. The wall stood until 1870, when it was replaced by the present iron railing.

Under Mr. Van Kleeck's rectorship, the parish was "at peace within itself," and his labors were abundantly blessed. There was a large accession to the number of communicants, and much interest was manifested in for-

St. George's Church.　　The Academy.　　House built by　　Flushing Institute.
Horse Shed.　　　　　　　　　　　Rev. Mr. Thorne.

FROM AN OLD PRINT—ABOUT 1840.

eign and domestic missions. For the first time in the existence of the parish, the juvenile portion took an active interest in missions. They sent out a box to the mission among the Indians at Green Bay, then almost outside of the western world. The Church at large had aroused from its lethargy in respect to its Divine commission to preach the Gospel to every creature. In 1835 the high stand was taken that every baptized member of the Church was a member of Christ's great missionary society. The wave extended over the whole Church. It reached the quiet waters of Flushing. In 1837, the rector reported to the convention $105 for Foreign Missions, and $202 for Domestic and Diocesan Missions At that same convention, the rector reported a large increase in the size of the congregation, that all the pews were taken and many more required, and that the vestry was taking active measures for an immediate enlargement of the church. Preliminary steps were taken toward this enlargement when the work was suspended for a time, by the unexpected resignation of the rector. Its completion belongs to the history of his successor.

At a vestry meeting, November 3, 1837, Mr. Van Kleeck tendered his resignation. He had received a call to St. Paul's Church, Troy, then, as well as now, a large and important parish, where his field of usefulness would be greatly enlarged. The resignation was to take effect after the following Sunday, which would be the second anniversary of his coming into the parish. The vestry could not complain. The resignation was accepted.

Some may still remember Matthew Durlin, the sexton of those days, and James Quarterman, the choirmaster, and Andrew G. Loweree, the organist. We read, that, in 1837, it was by the vestry resolved : "That under existing circumstances we dispense with the organ unless played gratuitously."

It is interesting to note, that each of the three last-named rectors gave two sons to the ministry of the Church.

On December 6, 1837, the Rev. Frederic J. Goodwin was elected to succeed Mr. Van Kleeck. The salary was fixed at $1,000. Mr. Goodwin was yet young in the ministry, and Flushing was his first charge.

THE REV. FREDERIC J. GOODWIN, D. D.

The enlargement of the church, to afford more pews, was a pressing need to which no prudent vestry could be indifferent. The parish was comparatively strong, numerically and financially, and was fully able to supply the need. But there was a resource in those days which sometimes tended to impair self-dependence. It was a resort to Trinity Church, New York. It was not to the credit of St. George's, that, on February 19, 1838, its vestry resolved : " That we apply to Trinity Church for aid in building an addition to the church. Resolved, that a petition be drawn up and signed by the clerk." If this petition was ever received, it seems to have been consigned to an unbroken slumber by the Committee on Appropriations, of Trinity.*

In April of that year a far more creditable record is made. It was resolved by the vestry : "That an addition of seventeen and a half feet be put on the church, and that Isaac Peck, Robert Carter and Jehiel Jaggar be a committee to attend to the building of the same." At the same meeting a resolution was passed, founded on an old and well worn text : " Resolved, that any pewholder deficient in paying his yearly rent, shall be considered as relinquishing his right to the same, and that the pew committee be instructed to relet it."

The work on the addition to the church was carried on with energy. The means were forthcoming. Among the contributors appear the names of Gardiner H. Howland, $200 ; Robert Carter, $200 ; Jehiel Jaggar, $200 ; Peter Ousterman, $100 ; Isaac Peck, $100 ; Estate of James Bloodgood, by Thomas Bloodgood, $100 ; Ladies' Missionary Society, $110. Two pews were paid for in advance, thus adding $100 to the fund. Twenty-six pews were added by the extension. The work was done by the late David Waters. Before the summer had passed, the congregation occupied their enlarged church, and had paid for it.

But, by a well-known law, an addition brings a de-

---

*Disosway, in his " Early Churches of New York," states that, between the years 1707 and 1800, Trinity parish gave to St. George's, Flushing, $21,750.

mand for new furnishings. The organ was antiquated, well worn by long use, and its capacity for sound was very feeble. A new and more powerful instrument was required. Nearly $700 were raised, and Mr. Jardine was called upon to build an organ at that price. A new and fine-toned instrument, in due time, took the place of its

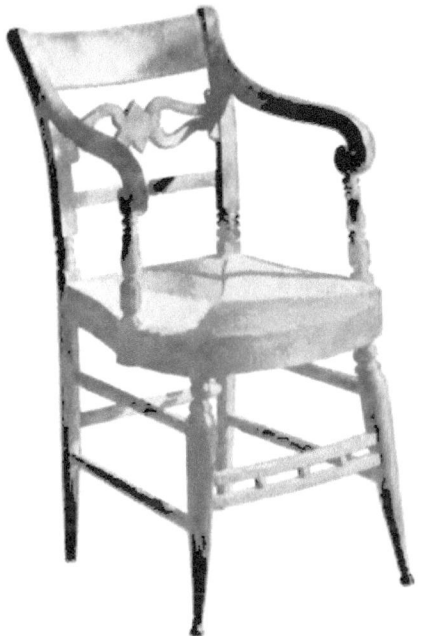

CHANCEL CHAIR, USED BEFORE 1838.

predecessor. Such is a brief history of the second organ of St. George's Church. It served well its purpose until superseded by a new one in 1862. But a new organ was not the only want. The chairs in the chancel were two old armchairs, rush seated and belonging to a past generation. They were probably used in the old church, torn down in 1820. These chairs were recently restored, missing parts added and are now in the vestry room of the church (page 117). On the extension of the church building, 1838, they were succeeded by two large armchairs of mahogany and hair cloth, which came unexpectedly. In October, 1838, a letter was received from some gentlemen, boarding at the Pavilion, stating that they had presented to the church two armchairs for the use of the chancel. The letter was signed by James T. Talman, L. A. Mills, B. A. Yarrington, Adolphus Lane and William W. Valk, M. D. This unexpected gift was acknowledged by the vestry, with a vote of thanks and "best wishes for their future happiness and welfare." These chairs also have been restored and placed in the vestry room.

An entry in an old book, kept by the church treasurer in 1838, reads : "Paid, bill for marble slab, $6.45." This is all that is extant of the history of the holy table in use when the writer came to the parish. It is now in the sanctuary, and is used as a credence, for the more convenient celebration of the Holy Communion. Of the older holy table nothing definite can be discovered. The ravages of time and human thoughtlessness have left no vestige of it.

About this time a rectory was built. It may be remembered that, during Mr. Van Kleeck's rectorship, preliminary steps were taken; but his resignation, and the financial difficulties of the parish, arrested further progress. Mr. Goodwin came to St. George's in December, and was married to a most estimable young lady of Flushing early in the following May. Hence the need of a rectory. A site was found in a plot fronting on Jamaica avenue, and extending in the rear to Madison

street. The ground was owned by Robert Carter, Isaac
Peck and Jehiel Jaggar. These gentlemen deeded to the
parish what was equivalent to two village lots. A gore of
land, formed by the junction of Jamaica and Madison
avenues, belonged to another party. Four gentlemen
bought this and gave it to the parish. A large and suitable building was erected and was used as a rectory for

ST. GEORGE'S RECTORY,—1838–1852.

some years. It is now owned by Mrs. Dr. Leggett's
estate, and is occupied by the "United Workers."

In July, 1842, the young rector broke down under his
many duties. He asked his vestry for leave of absence
for six months, to regain his strength, and recover from
an attack of bronchitis. The Rev. B. C. C. Parker, a son
of Bishop Parker, of Massachusetts, supplied his place.

Mr. Parker's ministrations were acceptable, and he was long well remembered by the congregation.

Although Mr. Goodwin returned with renewed health and vigor, the long pastorate he anticipated and his people desired, was not permitted. Severe afflictions, which came in startling and rapid succession, made a change necessary for his stricken household, as well as for himself. Under date of January, 16, 1844, he wrote : "Gentlemen of the Vestry : From the peculiarly afflictive and numerous bereavements my family have experienced during the past few months, they can not but deem a change of residence essential. In this opinion I fully concur. I yield, therefore, to the necessity of the case, and am constrained respectfully to ask your action, by releasing me from my present engagement as the Rector of St. George's Church. A change of residence will remove us from the sad scenes of our desolating bereavements. I can assure you that, wherever it shall be the pleasure of our Master to call me hereafter to exercise my ministry, I shall never cease to cherish the fond recollection of my labors here, and the many cheering incidents and affectionate endearments which give so lively an interest to the remembrance of the people of my first charge." The vestry, in response, unanimously resolved : "That we hereby record our sincere sympathy for our mourning and beloved rector and his family, in their repeated and peculiarly afflictive bereavements, and we assure him of our sense of the propriety and expediency of his course, in seeking a change of residence : That we convey to him, with much emotion, prompted by his zealous and efficient services, our deep regret at parting with a beloved pastor and spiritual guide, our faithful counsellor and friend, who has so greatly endeared himself to us all."

After his resignation, Mr. Goodwin removed to Middle-

town, Conn., and became the rector of the old and important parish in that city.   He continued there until his
death, February, 1872.   He was buried within the pre-
cincts of St. George's church-yard, Flushing, and beneath
the shadow of the old church in which he began his active ministry.

THE REV. GEORGE BURCKER.

Soon after Mr. Goodwin's resignation, the vestry elected
the Rev. George Burcker, of Flatbush, Long Island, " rector for two years, at a salary of $600 per year, commenc-
ing on March 1, 1844."   The vestry piously added that
the call was made for two years " in the hope that, by the
blessing of God on the church through the labors of their

minister, they would be able to advance the salary after
that time, if found requisite." The understanding was,
that if he occupied the rectory (worth a rental of $200),
a hundred dollars were to be deducted from his salary.
As rector he had a right, in common law, to occupy a
parsonage built expressly for the purpose. It was a vir-
tual reduction of fifty per cent. of the salary his predecessor had received. It is an act of justice, as well as a
part of the history, to say, that this retrenchment on the
part of the vestry seemed to them a necessity. By death
and removal, many liberal supporters of the parish had
been taken away. Financial stress and disaster had cut
off the generous and ready response of others. The vestry feared to mortgage an uncertain future. In the death
of a church warden, Mr. Robert Carter, the parish had,
during the year, lost one of its faithful friends and very
liberal supporters.

Mr. Burcker began his ministry in Flushing, in March,
1844. During the period of his labors, the spiritual health
and vigor of the parish were unchanged, depressed as it
was financially. Soon after he came, the record of a
noteworthy action on the part of the vestry appears.
With questionable wisdom it was resolved : "That the
pew rents, from the first of May next, shall be from three
to twelve dollars, the intermediate prices to be fixed by
the pew committee." For three years the vestry seemed
to live in peace and quietness. The meetings were few.
The reappointment of Matthew Durlin as sexton, at $65
per year, and the voting an annual gratuity of $25 to Mr.
Louis Yander and his amiable wife, for valuable and gra-
tuitous services at the organ and in the choir, about make
up the sum of the record. Nothing appears of the rector's reappointment, after the two years' limit of his
call. No mention was made of the advance of salary,

" if found requisite," or even of an inquiry as to its sufficiency.

Early in June, 1847, in the midst of good health and activity, the rector was stricken by a malady, in its nature fatal and of speedy termination. A few days of heroic suffering ended the life of the young pastor. The event, so sudden and sad, profoundly moved the congregation and the whole community. Every one, without respect of creed or race, showed great sorrow at his sudden death. All business was suspended during the hours of his funeral.

Mr. Burcker was yet young in his ministry. He had not great power of intellect or brilliancy as a preacher, but the simple power of goodness had widened his reputation far beyond the circle in which he lived. A number of the leading and representative clergy, from New York and Brooklyn, came to his funeral. The Rev. Dr. Whitehouse, of St. Thomas's, New York, afterward the Bishop of Illinois, preached on the occasion. A meeting of the clergy, presided over by Dr. Anthon, of St. Mark's, New York, was held. Resolutions were adopted, expressing their sorrow and the sense of loss which the Church at large, the parish of St. George's, and they had sustained in the death of their beloved brother ; and stating that the remembrance of his holy life, his faithful ministry, his serene and triumphant death would incite them to renewed diligence and devotion in the ministry. Similar resolutions were passed by the vestry, bearing testimony to his " labors, his consistent and devoted life, his simplicity and the graces that adorned his character, his love to God as exhibited by his love to man." "The closing scenes of his life," the resolutions described " as the embodiment of Christian faith, the triumph of Christian warfare, and his last words the great sermon of his life—the summing up and application of all his able and faithful teachings."

A mural tablet, erected by the women of the parish soon after his death, is in the chancel, with this text : "Whose faith follow, considering the end of his conversation, Jesus Christ." This was suggested, as the best description of his life and work, by his early friend and successor. This tablet, with the remembrances of the few who knew and loved him, is about all that remains of him among earthly things.   "So soon passeth it away, and we are gone." The enduring record is on high, written in the book of God's everlasting remembrance.

CHAPTER XVII.

AT a meeting of the vestry, held July 5, 1847, it was
resolved that the Rev. Thomas F. Fales, of Bruns-
wick, Maine, be called as minister of St. George's Church,
Flushing, for two years, at a salary of $600 per year and
the use of the parsonage." At the next vestry meeting,
September 21, 1847, the clerk reported: "That, in accordance with instructions, he had written an invitation
to Mr. Fales to become rector of the parish, and that he
had received an answer, reluctantly declining the call."
The Rev. Thomas F. Fales afterward accepted a call to
Waltham, Massachusetts, where he still lives as rector,
emeritus, of the parish.

At the same meeting of the vestry, the following action
was taken: "It was then, on motion, resolved that we
proceed to the election of a minister. Whereupon it was
unanimously resolved, that the Rev. J. Carpenter Smith,
Rector of Trinity Church, Rockaway, be called as Minister of St. George's Church, Flushing, at a salary of $600."
Mr. Smith accepted the call, and entered upon his duties
in Flushing, on the first Sunday in November, 1847.

The Rev. John Carpenter Smith was born in the town
of South Oyster Bay, Queens County, Long Island, in
1816, of Quaker parentage. He was, however, brought
up under the influence of the Church, in St. Ann's parish,

Brooklyn. He was educated at Kenyon College, Gambier, Ohio, and received his degree of A. B. from that institution in 1839.* He studied theology at the General Theological Seminary in New York City, and was ordained deacon, July 3, 1842, by the Rt. Rev. Benjamin T. Onderdonk, D.D., Bishop of New York He spent his deaconate in Ohio, as minister in charge of St. James's

THE REV. J. CARPENTER SMITH, 1847.

Church, Wooster. He was advanced to the priesthood, June 13, 1843, by Bishop McIlvaine. In 1844, he accepted a call to the rectorship of Trinity Church, Rockaway, Long Island. Here he remained until his removal to Flushing, November 1, 1847.

Mr. Smith began his ministry in St. George's parish, Flushing, with a salary of $600 a year. As one of the

*His degree of S. T. D. was conferred on him, by Columbia College, in 1860.

indications of the growth of the parish under his care,
and also as an indication that the parish has appreciated
his untiring devotion to its welfare, it is pleasant to record that the vestry gave him an additional $100 at the
end of his first year, and has, from time to time, increased
his salary—as often as the resources of the parish would
permit. This was done in 1854, in 1855 ("in acknowl-
edgment of the constant and unwearied labors and devotion" of the rector), and again in 1865. In 1871 we
find it recorded that it was by the vestry unanimously resolved : " Now, when brighter prospects are dawning
and the affairs of the parish are in a more sound and
flourishing condition than they have been for many years,
his vestry deem it an act of common justice, not only to
tender, but absolutely to insist on his receiving a small
addition to his present income." This last increase of
salary, however, Dr. Smith positively declined to accept
—deeming it more than the parish could well afford to
pay.

Early in 1850, a committee of three was appointed by
the vestry, "(1) to inquire as to the propriety of enlarging the church edifice ; (2) the best plan for such enlargement ; (3) its probable cost; and (4), the most suitable
mode of raising the necessary funds.' The chair appointed Isaac Peck, Sr., William Roe and Allan Macdonald. The committee reported in March, 1850, in favor of
the enlargement. Whereupon it was resolved : " That
St. George's Church be enlarged, by extending the two
sides thereof about twelve feet, so as to provide a row of
pews and an additional aisle on each side of the present
building." A building committee was appointed, to
" carry out the above resolution with all reasonable dis-
patch." A committee was also appointed " to raise the
funds needed." On April 10. 1850, the committee re-

ported that the expense of carrying into effect the enlargement would probably amount to $2,000, or $2,225. The matter was given back to the committee, with instructions to consider some plan of enlargement which would not exceed $1,000, or at most $1,200. Another member was added to the committee to aid in this task. He had some architectural skill and thought it might be done. A light iron gallery around the interior was sug-

ST. GEORGE'S CHURCH, BUILT 1854 — THE CHANCEL WAS BUILT 1891.

gested by a member of the vestry. The committee reported at the next meeting. They had drawn a plan and had brought the builder's estimates. It would cost $2,150. They could devise no enlargement for $1,200. After long discussion, they were instructed to "contract for the enlargement according to the plan and specifications, as soon as the necessary funds were raised for the purpose."

The committee was tardy in raising the "necessary funds for the purpose." At the next vestry meeting, held in September, 1850, they reported that "the funds for enlarging the church had not been raised, and as the summer was far advanced, they awaited the further order of the vestry." That order was soon given. On motion, it was resolved that "their report be received, and the committee be discharged." The author of the plan of enlargement resigned forthwith as a member of the vestry. The vestry accepted his resignation, and adjourned, after voting a present of $100 to the rector, and a three weeks' vacation in which to spend it.

This looks like a step backwards, but it was really a step forward, and a long one toward a new church. The plan of enlargement was not popular in the congregation, and the subject of a new edifice was being agitated. At a meeting of the vestry, April 14, 1851, the two church wardens, Jehiel Jaggar and Isaac Peck, Sr., and Allan Macdonald were appointed as a committee " to confer with the congregation on the subject of additional pew room in St. George's Church." It was soon discovered that the congregation desired a new church.

At a meeting of the vestry, held April 19, 1852, Isaac Peck, W. H. Schermerhorn and Allan Macdonald were appointed a committee " to take into consideration and to report to the vestry a suitable plan for such building with the cost, and the practicability of carrying the same into execution." There was a preamble to this resolution which reveals the cause of this bold action. That preamble was : "A general subscription having been circulated by some ladies, under the informal advice of the vestry, for the purpose of erecting a new church edifice, it was resolved"—as above. Some earnest women had come forward and offered their services. They would see what could be done by a voluntary subscription. If they could raise a certain amount, the vestry would be pledged to proceed in the work. More than the sum fixed upon was the result of their efforts. The vestry acknowledged its obligation and resolved: "That the thanks of this vestry be presented to Mrs. E. H. Mac-

THE REV. FRANCIS L. HAWKS, D. D.

donald, Mrs. Mary R. Pell and their associates, for their personal efforts in collecting subscriptions to build a new church edifice for St. George's Church, Flushing."

From that time the work was carried rapidly forward. The vestry held meetings weekly. A contract was made for the removal of the old church building "to the spot

now (then) occupied by the old horse shed." This was
May 17, 1852. On the 23d of that month, Wills and
Dudley, architects in New York, submitted two designs,
with estimates, for a new church—one with a tower and
spire at the (ecclesiastical) west end, at the estimated
cost of $17,000 ; the other, with a tower at the corner of
the front, and with a larger seating capacity, at a cost of
$16,000. The first plan was chosen—substantially like
the present church. The spire was to be omitted and
eight feet were to be taken from the chancel, to lessen the
cost. It was to be left to some future congregation to add
both at their will. The spire, by some means, was erected
with the tower, but the chancel remained forty years before its present extension. The blue granite of Horse-
neck (Greenwich), Conn., was wisely chosen by the vestry as the stone to be used. Before the removal of the
older building, a fraternal letter was received by the vestry from the Consistory of the Reformed Church, bidding
them God speed in their work, and offering the use
of the Reformed Church, Sunday afternoons. The offer
was gratefully accepted. Until the following September, services were held there in the afternoon, and in
the morning in the chapel at Whitestone. By that time,
the old church had been moved to its present site, on
Lincoln street, and made ready for use.

The foundation of the new church was completed early
in May, 1853. On the 18th of that month, the corner-
stone was laid by the Rev. Dr. William H. Lewis, and
the Rector delivered a historical address. The box deposited in the corner-stone contained a copy of the Holy
Bible, the Book of Common Prayer, the Flushing Journal of
last date, the latest Church papers, the Journal of the New
York Diocesan Convention for 1852, coins of the United
States, together with a list of the officers of the parish.

ST. PAUL'S CHAPEL, COLLEGE POINT, BUILT 1800.

The rectory, at the corner of Jamaica avenue and Madison street, was sold to Mrs. Mary Rodman Pell for $6,000, on November 29, 1852. After paying a mortgage of $2,000, the remaining $4,000 were placed to the credit of the building fund. Early in the next year, $12,000 were borrowed on three lots in New York City. Trinity parish, New York, agreed to become security for the payment of the interest, appropriating $400 a year for four years for that purpose—"provided that said church [i. e., St. George's] shall give its bond to this corporation, with an assignment of the rents of said lots as collateral, and that there shall be no reduction of the salary and emoluments of the rector or minister of said church, caused by the necessity of paying the interest on said debt, or otherwise."

The church was completed in May, 1854, at a cost of $32,222.80. The old bell, with additional metal, was recast into a larger one—the expense being borne by William H. Aspinwall and John Aspinwall, grandsons of the John Aspinwall who gave the first bell to the parish. The spire, as first completed, was topped by a flattened sphere. This a kindly storm removed from its position, before the scaffolding was taken down, and the cross was substituted according to the original plan of the architects.

On Wednesday, May 31, 1854, the sale of pews took place in the church—purchasers paying eight per cent. of the value of the pews, for ground rent. Twenty-seven pews were sold—the highest price paid being $300, the lowest $100, and the highest premium for choice $100. The whole sum received from the sale of pews, and from the premiums on pews let, was $6,751.60.

The new St. George's Church was consecrated on the first day of June, 1854, by the Rt. Rev. Jonathan M. Wainwright, D. D., D. C. L., Provisional Bishop of the

Diocese of New York. The Rev. Dr. Hawks, rector of St. Thomas's Church, New York, preached the sermon. Among the clergy present, were the Rev. Dr. William H. Moore, of Hempstead ; the Rev. Dr. William S. Johnson, of Jamaica ; the Rev. George A. Shelton, of Newtown. Thus all of the old colonial churches of Queens County were represented. The church was filled to its utmost seating capacity. The distinguished preacher took for his text the words: "Worship God." Rev. 22 : 9. The sermon was the first one preached in the pulpit of the new St. George's Church. No sermon since has excelled it.

CHAPTER XVIII.

RECTORSHIP OF THE REV. J. CARPENTER SMITH, S. T. D. A. D. 1854–1897.

AFTER the completion of the new church, in 1854, the vestry was able to attend to the appeals of the inhabitants of Clintonville (now Whitestone). The rector was authorized, in July, 1855, to call the Rev. William Short, as an assistant minister—to serve Clintonville and its neighborhood. In the same year, we read that the experiment was tried of taking quarterly, instead of weekly, collections in the church for parish expenses. This experiment was abandoned the next year, because the result fell " far short of the hopes of the vestry."

In 1857, the vestry found itself responsible for a debt of about $15,000—most of which had been incurred in building the new church—and, seeing no other prospect of reducing it, resolved to part with some of its New York real estate. The lot number 125 Chambers street was accordingly sold, for $16,500, to James Boorman, who, at the time, held an unexpired lease of the property. The receipt of a legacy of $4,000 from the estate of Miss Emma M. Jaggar, during the same year, enabled the vestry to make better provision for the Sunday School. It was at first resolved to pull down the old chapel and build a new one, but during the next year this plan was abandoned. The old addition of seventeen feet, at the rear of the chapel, was removed and rebuilt—thus pro-

THE REV. J. CARPENTER SMITH, S. T. D.

viding the three class rooms, which are still so useful—
and the whole building was put in thorough repair. This
was a wise decision, for no building could have been
erected for $4,000 that would take the place of our com-
modious and quaint old chapel. The total cost of these
improvements was $4,424.82.

The mission at Whitestone, with the consent of the
Rector, Wardens and Vestrymen of St. George's parish,
became an independent parish in 1858. Permission
was granted, on condition that the new parish forever relinquish all claim to a share in the property of St. George's
parish.

This appears to have been a period of great missionary
activity in the parish, for early in the next year, March,
1859, we read that several gentlemen had bought a lot
and built a chapel at the head of the Vleigh, and offered
to transfer the property to St. George's parish. The records give us no information why the property—now
known as Pell's Chapel—was never accepted. During
the same year, Spencer H. Smith and William E. Chisolm
waited on the vestry, concerning the proposal to erect a
chapel at Strattonport—now College Point. This chapel
was completed in May, 1860, at a cost of $3,000, and was
consecrated in 1861. The lot was the gift of Conrad
Poppenhousen. The vestry recorded its thanks to W.
E. Chisolm, Frederic A. Potts, Henry A. Bogert, Spencer
H. Smith and Mrs. Joseph Harris King, for services in
connection with the erection of St. Paul's Chapel.

In 1863, the brief record that the rector was granted a
vacation of six months to recover his health, together with
a similar record in 1872, tells us something of the effect
of the exacting duties of a growing parish.

During all this period, and, indeed, down to the present time, scarcely a year has passed during which we do

not find on the records of the vestry, complaint about
the non-payment of pew rents.   The vestry passed resolutions, appointed committees, issued circular letters,
threatened time after time to dispossess the delinquents,
etc., etc., but the evil was not removed.   People insisted
on retaining the use of pews to the exclusion of all others, but refused to pay for such privilege.

St. George's Brotherhood was organized in 1870 and
has, therefore, now completed twenty-seven years of ac-

TOWN FARM MISSION.

tive work in the parish.   The minutes of the first meeting read as follows : "On the evening of Thursday, January 27, 1870, a half-dozen members of the parish of St.
George's, Flushing, N. Y., met informally in the chapel,
to consider the propriety of forming an organization for
Church work in the parish.   J. Carpenter Smith, S. T. D.,
the rector, was invited to act as chairman and L. B.
Prince appointed secretary.   Those present were—Rev.
Dr. Smith, Rev. Mr. Kimber, Martin H. Roberts, Fanning

C. Tucker, Lindley M. Franklin, Burrall Hoffman, Isaac
Russell. L. Bradford Prince. The meeting was opened
with prayer. After determining that the name of the organization should be the St. George's Brotherhood, the
meeting adjourned to Thursday evening, February 3,
1870."

The Brotherhood was incorporated April 12, 1871.
The objects of the organization, as stated in the "Act of
Incorporation," are : To diffuse and extend religious
knowledge ; to carry on missionary operations ; to afford
charitable relief to the aged, the infirm, the orphan and
the destitute ; to establish a library of religious books ;
to assist in the education of candidates for the ministry ; to promote the general prosperity, of the parish.
The Sunday School, which had been established at Black
Stump about eight years before, and the Church services,
which had been carried on at the Town Farm for about
three years, were placed under the care of the Brotherhood. The two missions were later consolidated and
continued at the Town Farm until a few months ago,
when the sale of the farm made it necessary to move to
another house in the neighborhood. In 1872, the Brotherhood took up the work at Queens, which had been in-
augurated by the Rev. Thomas Cook, of Jamaica, and
continued it until the Cathedral assumed the responsibility. The Brotherhood also assisted the College Point
mission for a number of years. It established a mission
at Bayside in 1874. The Rev. George R. Van De Water,
D. D., Rector of St. Andrew's Church, New York, then a
member of the Brotherhood, was the first lay-reader at
Bayside. This work at Bayside was continued by the
Brotherhood until 1892, when the parish of All Saints'
Bayside, was incorporated. All Saints' Church was built
under the auspices of the Brotherhood in 1892, in accord-

ALL SAINT'S CHURCH, BAYSIDE, BUILT 1872.

ance with plans furnished by J. King James—then a member of the Brotherhood. The money was raised partly in Bayside and partly in Flushing.

In 1871, the church, which had now been in constant use for seventeen years, was closed for repairs during the summer, and service was held in the Town Hall. The roof was re-slated at a cost of $1,475, the interior of the church was renovated and the walls were decorated.

In 1878, Walter Bowne, who had long been a vestry-man, and a generous supporter of all parish work, died, leaving a bequest of $5,000, to be used in building a rec-tory. John W. Lawrence gave the lot, and the present rectory, at 45 Locust street, was completed during the next year.

At the death of Dr. Abraham Bloodgood, in 1880, the parish received from his wife's estate the sum of $5,000 —to be added to the endowment fund. Mrs. Bloodgood had died eleven years before, and had left the parish $1,200, requesting her husband, at his death, to make provision for the larger bequest.

The lease on lot number 116 Chambers street, New York, expired in 1884, and was renewed for a period of twenty-one years, at an annual rental of $1,000. This increase in income—the former rental of the property had been $150 a year—enabled the vestry to make some de-sired improvements in the chancel of the church, at a cost of $820. The present altar and reredos were at this time placed in the church.

On the seventh day of November, 1887, Dr. Smith com-pleted the fortieth year of his rectorship. The event was celebrated by a reception at the rectory, when the whole community assembled to offer their congratulations.

The names of the various assistants, who have served under Dr. Smith, will be found in an appendix. In 1889,

the rector and the vestry decided that some permanent
arrangement should be made to relieve the rector of a
part of his many and exacting duties.   The Rev. Henry
D. Waller was, therefore, called to the position of assistant minister in the parish, with the right of succession to
the rectorship; and the rector formally resigned to him
certain duties and privileges which, in effect, gave him
the joint care of the parish.   The call was accepted, and

ST. GEORGE'S RECTORY, BUILT 1879.

Mr. Waller entered on his duties, Whitsunday, June 7,
1889.

In 1894 the chancel of the church was pulled down to
make room for a larger one and, at the same time, the
whole church was thoroughly renovated.   The north
porch was built at this time, and the organ was removed
from the gallery, rebuilt, and placed on the left side of the
chancel.   The building committee, in charge of these im-

THE NEW CHANCEL, BUILT 1504.

provements, consisted of the two church wardens—George Pople and Dr. J. W. Barstow, and three vestrymen—E. V. W. Rossiter, F. L. Goodwin and F. S. Beecroft. The architect was J. King James. The total cost of the improvements was $29.152.82. The work was begun in May, and the new chancel was consecrated on the second Sunday in Advent, December 9, 1894, by the Rt. Rev. Leighton Coleman, S. T. D., LL. D., Bishop of Delaware —the Bishop of the diocese being abroad at the time. At this first service in the new chancel, the vested choir of men and boys was introduced. It has rendered acceptable service ever since.

The first Sunday of next November, 1897, will mark the fiftieth anniversary of Dr. Smith's first service in St. George's Church. When he came to Flushing there were about 140 communicants in St. George's parish. To-day there are 770, although the parishes of Whitestone and Bayside have been built within the original parochial limits of the parish of Flushing. Both of these parishes were at first missions of St. George's Church. If we take into consideration the whole territory over which Dr. Smith was placed as rector, in 1847, we find that during the time of his incumbency the number of communicants has grown from 140 to 950.

The following items of information give the state of the parish to-day. The services at the parish church are under the care of the rector and his associate. At College Point is St. Paul's Chapel, under the care of the Rev. William Henry Barnes, rector's assistant. Emmanuel Chapel—formerly the Town Farm mission—and St. John's Chapel, Murray Hill, are under the care of the Brotherhood. In these two chapels, the services are generally conducted by lay-readers. The Murray Hill mission was begun by the Brotherhood in 1894. Services are at pres-

ent held in a rented building, but the Brotherhood has purchased a large lot on Sanford avenue, extending from Wilson to Boerum avenue, where a chapel will eventually be built.

The endowment of the parish consists of two lots in New York City, which, at present, yield an income of $2,050 ; the Bloodgood fund of $5,000, which is invested from time to time by the vestry ; and the Peck fund of $500, the income of which is devoted to the care of the Peck grave-yard.   The lease of lot number 116 Chambers street, New York, will expire in 1902, and that of number 79 Warren street, in 1908.   In 1895, Mr. William H. Ewbank deeded to the parish a parcel of ground on the northwest corner of Main and Amity streets, together with the six houses which occupy the site—reserving for himself the income from this property during his life time.

May this exhibition of St. George's past history, its present opportunities, and its future possibilities, incite us all to renewed efforts and to more thorough consecration.

LAUS DEO.

APPENDIX.

I. Rectors.

1. *Patrick Gordon.................... A. D. 1702
2. William Urquhart................ A. D. 1704–1709
3. Thomas Poyer................... A. D. 1710–1731
4. Thomas Colgan................. A. D. 1733–1755
5. †Samuel Seabury............... A. D. 1757–1765
6. Joshua Bloomer................. A. D. 1769–1790
7. William Hammell............... A. D. 1790–1795
8. Elijah D. Rattoone.......... ... A. D. 1797–1802
9. Abram L. Clarke............... A. D. 1803–1809
10. Barzillai Buckley.............. A. D. 1809–1820
11. John V. E. Thorne............. A. D. 1820–1826
12. William A. Muhlenberg.......... A. D. 1826–1829
13. William H. Lewis.............. A. D. 1829–1833
14. J. Murray Forbes.............. A. D. 1833–1834
15. Samuel R. Johnson............ A. D. 1834–1835
16. Robert B. Van Kleeck.......... A. D. 1835–1837
17. Frederic J. Goodwin........... A. D. 1837–1844
18. George Burcker............... A. D. 1844–1847
19. J. Carpenter Smith........... A. D. 1847 ——

II. Assistant Ministers.

1. William Short.................. A. D. 1854–1858
2. Thomas A. Jaggar............ .... A. D. 1860–1862

*Gordon was appointed in 1702, but died just before his induction.
†This is the correct date of Mr. Seabury's induction. That on page 35 should agree with this.

ASSISTANT MINISTERS.—Continued.

3. Gustavus M. Murray . . . . A. D. 1862–1864
4. Augustine W. Cornell . . . . A. D. 1864–1865
5. P. W. Styker . . . . A. D. 1865–1868
6. Thomas Drumm . . . . A. D. —— 1868
7. Henry Webbe . . . . A. D. 1868–1869
8. Joshua Kimber . . . . A. D. 1869–1873
9. John F. Appleton . . . . A. D. 1871–1873
10. J. Frederick Esch . . . . A. D. 1873–1876
11. G. F. Behringer . . . . A. D. —— 1876
12. Joseph Beers . . . . A. D. 1878–1879
13. Edward H. True . . . . A. D. 1879–1889
14. Harold Arrowsmith . . . . A. D. 1879–1883
15. Williams Howland . . . . A. D. 1881–1882
16. William P. Brush . . . . A. D. 1883–1885
17. Robert S. Carlin . . . . A. D. 1886–1888
18. Henry D. Waller . . . . A. D. 1889 ——
19. William Du Hamel . . . . A. D. 1892–1895
20. William H. Barnes . . . . A. D. 1895 ——

III. WARDENS AND VESTRYMEN.

The dates given below mark the years when the wardens and vestrymen were first elected. Most of them served more than a year; many were re-elected, year after year, for periods of considerable length. The first two wardens and the first six vestrymen were appointed by the charter; all others were elected by the congregation.

WARDENS.

John Aspinwall	1761	Francis Lewis	1770
Thomas Grenell	1761	David Colden	1773
John Willet	1770	Robert Crommelin	1785

WARDENS.—Continued.

William Ustick	1787	James Scott	1833
Francis Lewis, Jr.	1791	Robert Carter	1837
Gerard G. Beekman	1795	Jehiel Jaggar	1849
John H. Smith	1796	Allan Macdonald	1854
Daniel Thorne	1800	William Roe	1860
William Prince	1804	Joseph Harris King	1862
John Hoogland	1806	John W. Lawrence	1867
Thomas Phillips	1809	Morris Franklin	1870
Daniel Bloodgood	1812	George Pople	1884
Isaac Peck	1829	J. W. Barstow, M. D.	1886
Thomas H. Thomas	1831	E. V. W. Rossiter	1896

VESTRYMEN.

John Dyer	1761	Francis Lewis, Jr.	1787
Christopher Robert	1761	John H. Smith	1787
John Morell	1761	John B. Hicks	1791
Joseph Haviland	1761	Gerard G. Beekman	1794
Francis Brown	1761	Thomas Lowerie, Sr.	1795
Jeremiah Mitchell	1761	Thomas Lowerie, Jr.	1795
Christopher Robert	1770	William Prince, Jr.	1796
Thomas Hallett	1770	Louis Cornell	1798
Robert Crommelin	1770	Daniel Kissam	1800
Nathaniel Tom, Sr.	1770	John Hoogland	1800
William Lowrier	1770	David Gardener	1802
Robert Morrell	1770	Thomas Phillips	1803
Benjamin Thorn	1773	Thomas Ustick	1803
James Mackrell	1780	Samuel Van Wyck	1804
Thomas Fairchild	1780	Daniel Bloodgood	1804
Daniel Thorne	1785	Thomas Lawrence	1804
William Ustick	1785	Richard Platt	1805
Francis Lewis	1786	Benjamin Prince	1806
Lambert Moore	1787	James Bloodgood	1806

VESTRYMEN.—Continued.

Lawrence Roe	1807	James Macdonald, MD	1847
Matthew Farrington	1812	Joseph Trulock	1849
Joshua Cornell	1812	Walter Bowne	1849
Isaac Peck	1813	Allan Macdonald	1850
Thomas Marston	1816	Robert B. Carter	1850
Daniel Thorn Smith	1817	Charles R. Lincoln	1851
Walter Roe	1820	Charles H. Hamilton	1851
Watson E. Lawrence	1822	Wm. H. Schermerhorn	1851
Samuel Willet	1824	Joseph Harris King	1854
Winant Van Zandt	1826	George Bradish	1855
James Loweree	1826	Edward J. Mann	1855
James Lawrence	1826	J. Milnor Peck	1862
Thomas H. Thomas	1827	Peter R. Mumford	1864
Samuel Nicoll	1828	George Pople	1864
James Morrell	1829	Morris Franklin	1864
William Haughten	1829	James B. Brewster	1864
Joseph Bloodgood, MD	1829	William Stebbins, Jr.	1864
William Roe	1830	Charles A. Roe	1869
William Mitchell	1830	John Robinson	1870
Samuel G. Loweree	1831	Loomis L. White	1870
Ananias Langdon	1831	J. W. Barstow, M.D	1874
Alexander Varian	1831	Samuel D. Row	1874
Edwin Lawrence	1832	Isaac Bloodgood	1875
Peter Ousterman	1832	L. Murray Franklin	1880
James Scott	1833	E. M. Travers	1881
James Lawrence	1833	Effingh'm W. Lawrence	1883
Christopher Loweree	1835	Ezra F. Thompson	1883
Robert Carter	1836	David Richmond	1883
Jehiel Jaggar	1838	E. V. W. Rossiter	1883
John W. Lawrence	1838	Robert S. Tucker	1884
Elijah Peck	1841	John Henderson	1884
John M. E. Valk	1843	John W. Weed	1886

Vestrymen.—Continued.

James A. Renwick....1886   Joseph Fitch.........1893
Elisha H. Goodwin...1889   James Breath.........1894
D. Sheppard Jones....1889   Charles H. Garretson..1894
William T. Dobson...1890   George Webster Peck.1896
Frederick S. Beecroft..1893

www.ingramcontent.com/pod-product-compliance
Lightning Source LLC
Chambersburg PA
CBHW021124020726
47500CB00003B/905